Easy PowerPoint 4
for Windows

Bryan Pfaffenberger

Easy PowerPoint 4 for Windows

Copyright © 1994 by Que® Corporation

Library of Congress Catalog No.: 94-65337

ISBN: 1-56529-737-7

97   96   4

Interpretation of the printing code: the rightmost double-digit number is the year of the book's printing; the rightmost single-digit number, the number of the book's printing. For example, a printing code of 94-1 shows that the first printing of the book occurred in 1994.

Screen Reproductions in this book were created with Collage Plus from Inner Media, Inc., Hollis, NH.

Publisher: David P. Ewing

Associate Publisher: Corinne Walls

Publishing Director: Lisa A. Bucki

Managing Editor: Anne Owen

Product Marketing Manager: Greg Wiegand

Credits

Acquisitions Editor
Nancy Stevenson

Product Director
Steve Schaefer

Development/Production Editor
Jill D. Bond

Technical Editor
Jonathan Ruffy

Book Designer
Amy Peppler-Adams

Cover Designer
Jay Corpus

Production Team
Stephen Adams
Angela Bannan
Claudia Bell
Anne Dickerson
Jay Lesandrini
Elizabeth Lewis
Andrea Marcum
Nanci Sears Perry
Amy Steed
Michael Thomas

Indexer
Michael Hughes

Composed in *Stone Serif* and *MCPdigital* by Que Corporation

About the Author

Bryan Pfaffenberger is a Charlottesville, Virginia-based writer who teaches presentation graphics, oral communications, and the sociology of computing in organizations at the University of Virginia, where currently he is Associate Professor of Technology, Communications, and Culture.

Contents at a Glance

Contents

Part III: Working with Objects 80

Part IV: Working with Text 114

Part V: Working with Graphs and Visuals   148

Part VI: Fine-Tuning Your Presentation and Producing Media   172

Part VII: Sample Documents   196

Glossary   208

Index   210

Action Index

How To Use the Task Sections

The Task sections consist of numbered steps that tell you how to accomplish certain tasks, such as saving a workbook or filling a range. The numbered steps walk you through a specific example so that you can learn the task by actually doing it.

Big Screen

At the beginning of each task is a large screen shot that shows how the computer screen will look after you complete the procedure that follows in that task. Sometimes the screen shot shows a feature discussed in that task, however, such as a shortcut menu.

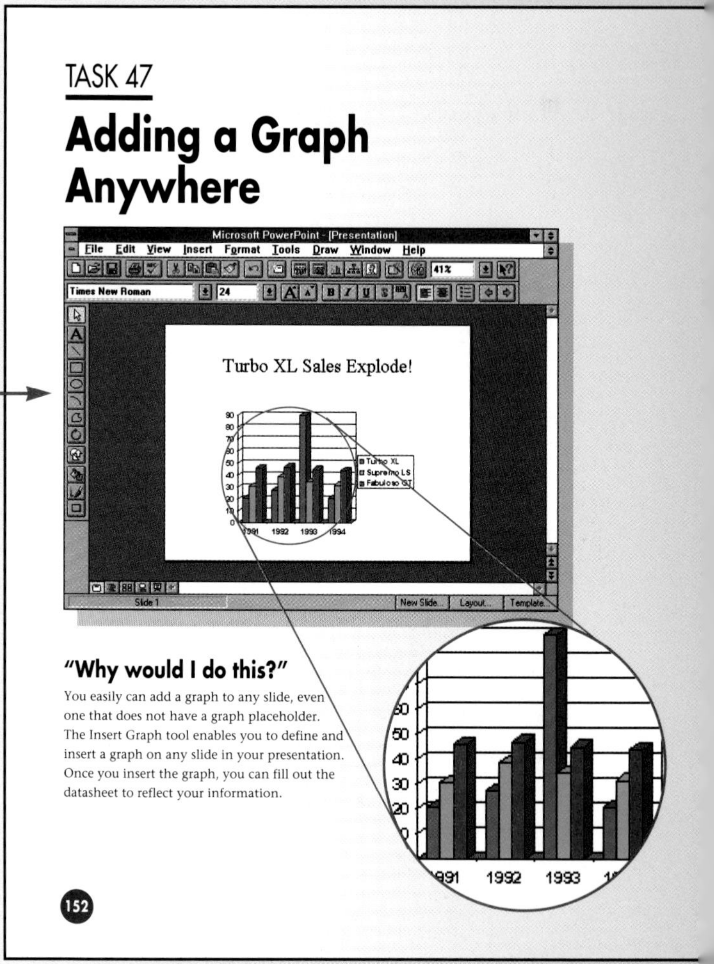

TASK 47

Adding a Graph Anywhere

Microsoft PowerPoint - [Presentation]

File Edit View Insert Format Tools Draw Window Help

Turbo XL Sales Explode!

"Why would I do this?"

You easily can add a graph to any slide, even one that does not have a graph placeholder. The Insert Graph tool enables you to define and insert a graph on any slide in your presentation. Once you insert the graph, you can fill out the datasheet to reflect your information.

152

Step-by-Step Screens

Each task includes a screen shot for each
step of a procedure. The screen shot shows
how the computer screen looks at each step
in the process.

1 Create a new slide with the Title Only
AutoLayout. Click the title text area and
type the title **Turbo XL Sales Explode!**
Now click the **Insert Graph** tool.
PowerPoint starts Microsoft Graph. You see
the sample chart and datasheet window.

NOTE ▼

To make more room for the row headings,
click the line dividing the first column and
column A; An arrow pointing both ways
indicates that you can now widen the
column. Drag right to make room
for the headings.

Notes

Many tasks include short notes that tell you a
little more about certain procedures. These
notes define terms, explain other options,
refer you to other sections (when applicable),
and so on.

2 To create your graph, you just modify the
sample data. To do this, click the cell in
row 1 containing the heading **East**. Type
the new heading. It automatically replaces
the existing heading. Press the **down
arrow** to edit the next heading. Do the
same for the third heading. To enter the
column headings, click the cell in column
A containing the heading **1st Qtr**. Type
the new heading, and then press
Tab to edit the next heading.
Just use the sample numbers
for the data.

3 Click the **Datasheet** tool on the toolbar
to hide the datasheet. This enables you to
see your graph. If you need to redisplay
the datasheet, click the **Datasheet** tool
again.

WHY WORRY?

If you accidentally click on the screen
but not on the graph and the Graph
toolbar disappears, just double-click
the graph again to display the Graph
toolbar.

153

Why Worry? Notes

You may find that you performed a task,
such as sorting data, that you didn't want to
do after all. The Why Worry? notes tell you
how to undo certain procedures or get out of
a situation, such as displaying a Help screen.

Introduction

Introduction

Do you have to give a presentation? Studies show that visual aids, such as overheads or 35mm slides, help your audience. With these aids, your audience remembers your message; they reach consensus faster; and they think you're more professional!

Microsoft PowerPoint can help you with your whole presentation. It does more than just help you create your presentation media, such as overheads. You can use PowerPoint to plan and organize your speech, too. When you've got everything just right, PowerPoint will even help you rehearse your presentation so that you can avoid getting cut short if you run out of time!

PowerPoint is easy to use, thanks to the program's built-in Wizards. When you create a presentation, the AutoContent Wizard enables you to choose from several well-designed presentation outlines that you can modify. The Pick a Look Wizard enables you to choose from more than a hundred professionally designed graphic layouts. You can easily find one that's just right for your style and your situation.

Specifically, *Easy PowerPoint 4 for Windows* shows you how to do the following:

- In Part I, you learn the basics of running this program, including starting PowerPoint, getting help, using menus, and using the windows. Many of these features closely resemble those in other Windows applications. If you are already familiar with them, just skip to Part II, "Creating a New Presentation," and get started on your first presentation right away!

- Part II shows you how to create a new presenation using the AutoContent Wizard. In PowerPoint, you create your presentation using just one file. It contains everything you need— an outline of your presentation, your slides, audience handouts, and even your speaker's notes. It gives you ideas on how to organize your presentation, too.

- Part III shows you how to work with objects, graphs, and clip art. All objects have certain features in common. You can select them independently of other objects on-screen. You can duplicate them if you want an exact copy of an object you've just created. You can resize and move objects, positioning them just where you want them. You can group them so that two or more objects move together. And you can enhance them by changing the object's *attributes*, such as line type, fill color, shadow, and embossing effect.

■ Part IV shows you how to work with text and add it anywhere in a presentation. PowerPoint takes care of much of the visual appeal automatically. When you attach a template to a PowerPoint presentation, the template specifies the font (design) of the text, as well as its size (in printer's points), its color, and its alignment (flush left or centered).

■ Part V shows you how to use Microsoft Graph, which is a business graph program that has many capabilities. If you're new to graphs, you might feel overwhelmed by all the Microsoft Graph options. But making a great-looking graph is easy. You just type your data in place of the sample data Graph provides. Thanks to Graph's AutoFormats, you don't have to worry about choosing formatting options. Graph does the work for you—all you need to do is choose the correct graph type for your data!

■ Part VI shows you how to ensure that your presentation meets professional standards and produce a variety of presentation media. With Slide Sorter, you can make sure that your slides are in the correct order—and if they're not, you can rearrange them easily. With the Change Case command, you can easily correct problems with inconsistent capitalization. With PowerPoint's spelling checker, you can make sure that your presentation won't contain an embarrassing spelling mistake. You can even have PowerPoint time your presentation so you won't risk getting cut off if you run over your allotted time.

■ Part VII provides sample PowerPoint documents that you can refer to for ideas and presentations.

■ Part VIII provides a reference section that includes a detailed glossary of terms used in PowerPoint and information about the PowerPoint screen and the toolbars.

PART I
Running PowerPoint

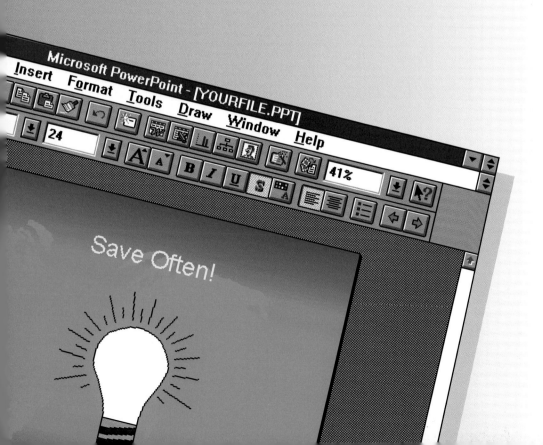

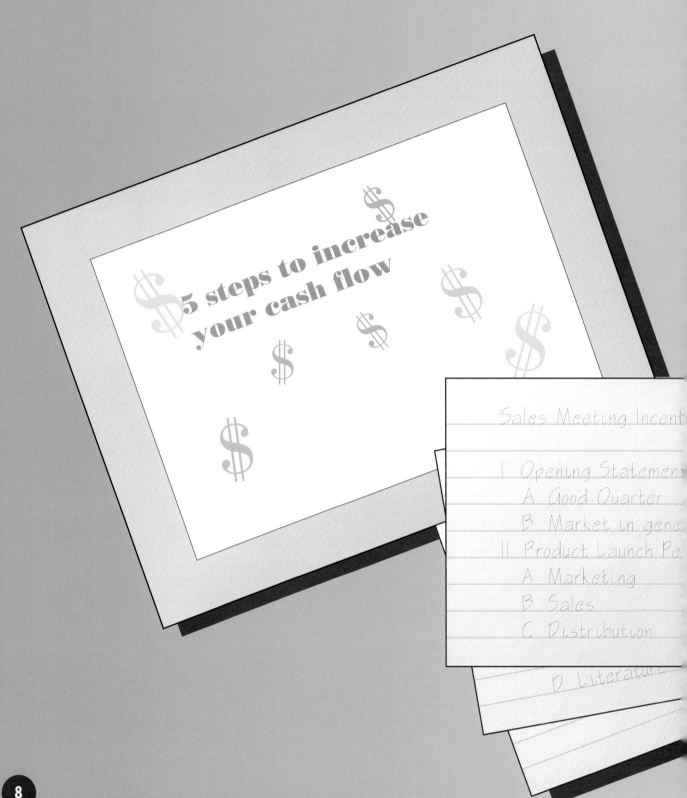

Do you have to give a presentation? Studies show that visual aids, such as overheads or 35mm slides, help your audience. With these aids, they remember your message. They reach consensus faster. And they think you're more professional!

Microsoft PowerPoint can help you with your whole presentation. It does more than just help you create your presentation media, such as overheads. You can use PowerPoint to plan and organize your speech, too. When you've got everything just right, PowerPoint will even help you rehearse your presentation, so that you can avoid getting cut short if you run out of time!

PowerPoint is easy to use, thanks to the program's built-in Wizards. When you create a presentation, the AutoContent wizard enables you to choose from several well-designed presentation outlines that you can modify. The Pick a Look wizard enables you to choose from more than a hundred professionally-designed graphic layouts. You easily can find one that's just right for your style and your situation.

In the first part of *Easy PowerPoint*, you learn the basics of running this program, including starting PowerPoint, getting help, using menus, and using the windows. Many of these features closely resemble those in other Windows applications. If you are already familiar with them, just skip to Part II, "Creating a New Presentation"— and get started on your first presentation right away!

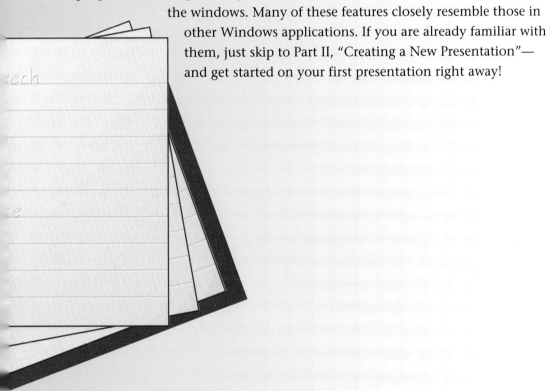

TASK 1

Starting and Quitting PowerPoint

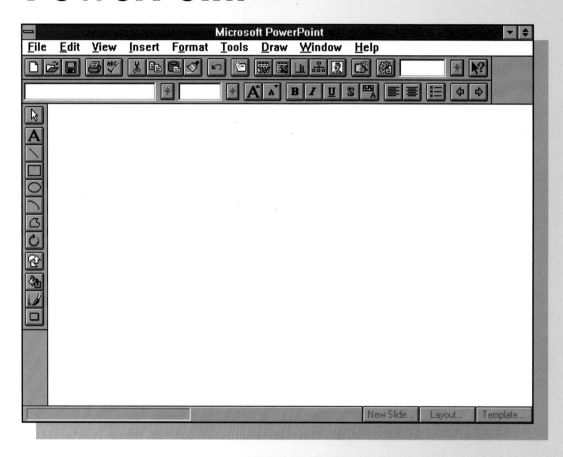

"Why would I do this?"

Like any computer program, you must start
PowerPoint in order to use it. When you finish
working with the program, you quit and return
to Windows. This task covers these basic skills.

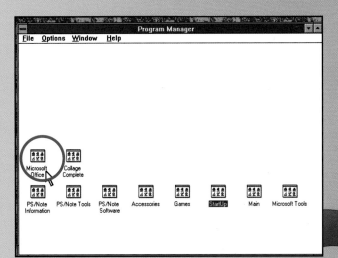

1 In Program Manager, move the mouse pointer to the program group that contains PowerPoint, and double-click the left mouse button. The program group application window appears. In this example, PowerPoint is in the Microsoft Office program group.

2 Move the pointer to the **Microsoft PowerPoint** icon, and double-click the left mouse button. Assuming that this is the first time you've run PowerPoint, you'll see the Quick Preview dialog box on-screen.

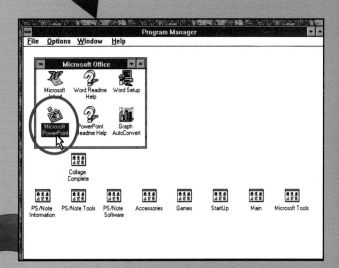

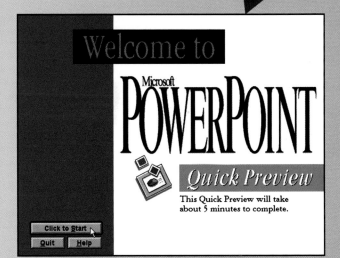

3 Click **Click to Start** to start Quick Preview. It gives a good overview of PowerPoint and takes only about five minutes. Just follow the easy on-screen instructions. When the Quick Preview is finished, you see PowerPoint again. The Tip of the Day dialog box appears which displays a different tip every time you start PowerPoint.

Task 1: Starting and Quitting PowerPoint

4 Move the mouse pointer to the **Next Tip** button or the **More Tips** if you want to see more of them, and click the left mouse button. To close the Tip of the Day dialog box, just move the pointer to **OK**, and click the left mouse button. The PowerPoint dialog box appears.

5 From this dialog box, you choose options for starting your presentation. For now, just close the dialog box by moving the pointer to **Cancel** and clicking the left mouse button.

> **NOTE** ▼
>
> With PowerPoint, you use the left mouse button for almost all clicking actions. From now on, we'll just say "click" rather than "move the pointer to something, and click the left mouse button." The right mouse button has some special features in PowerPoint. You learn about these features later.

6 Across the top you see the title bar. This contains the Control menu icon (the dash). When you click this dash, you see a menu that enables you to choose options for the PowerPoint window, as well as to switch to other applications. On the right you see the Minimize button. Click this to reduce PowerPoint to an icon. The Restore icon reduces PowerPoint's window to a smaller size, or full size.

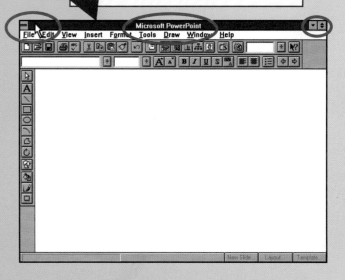

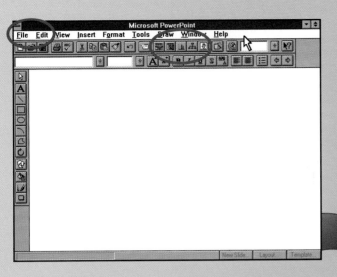

7 The menu bar contains menu names, which you can click to see menus containing commands. Below the menu bar is the Standard toolbar. Just by clicking these buttons, called *tools*, you can choose many of the commands you'll need to use.

8 This is the Formatting toolbar. You click these tools to change the appearance of text. On the right side of the screen is the Drawing toolbar. These tools help you create artwork.

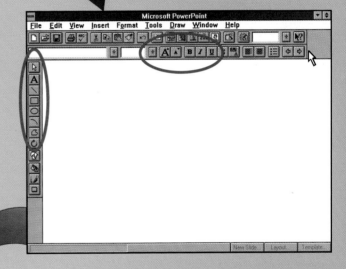

9 This is the status bar. Helpful information appears here. For example, when you move the mouse pointer to a command or tool, the Status bar tells what it does. To quit PowerPoint, just double-click the Control menu icon (the big dash in the upper left corner of the screen). You see Program Manager again.

Getting Help

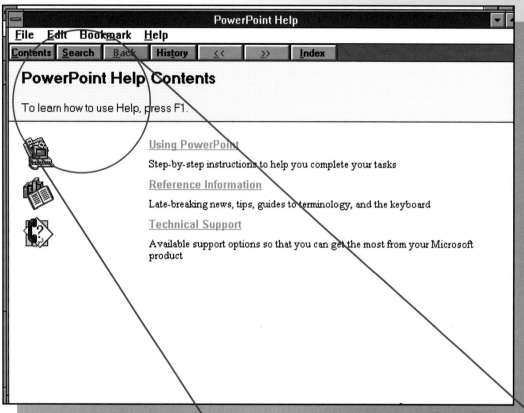

"Why would I do this?"

PowerPoint is a professional presentation graphics program with many complex features. A new user easily can feel overwhelmed, but relax. With PowerPoint, you easily can get help, right on the screen. In this task, you learn how to use PowerPoint's help capabilities.

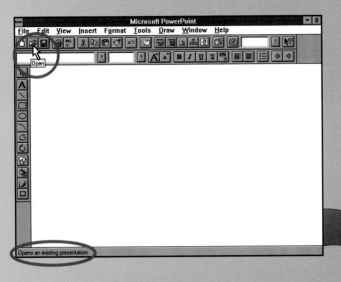

1 Start PowerPoint, and close the Tip and PowerPoint dialog boxes. Now move the mouse pointer to one of the tools, and leave the tip on the tool for a moment. You see a ToolTip that gives the name of the tool. Also, look at the status bar. This tells what the tool does.

2 On the right side of the Standard toolbar, you find the **Help** tool. Click this now. The mouse pointer becomes a big question mark. When you click something with the question mark pointer, you see Help about what you've clicked.

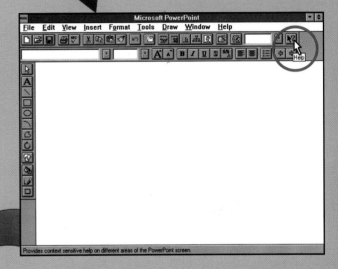

3 With the pointer showing the question mark shape, click the **Save** tool. You see a Help page that tells what the Save tool does. Actually, it tells what the Save command on the File menu does. The tool is a shortcut to this menu command.

Task 2: Getting Help

4 Note the underlined text in the Help page. These are called *jumps*. If you click one, you see the Help page with that title. Try clicking **Saving Presentations**. You see more information about saving your PowerPoint presentation.

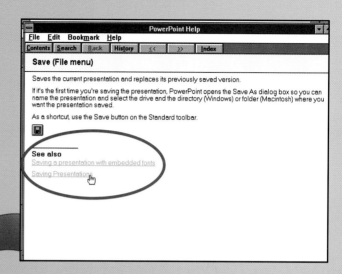

5 To see the Help Contents, just click the **Contents** button. You see the Contents page.

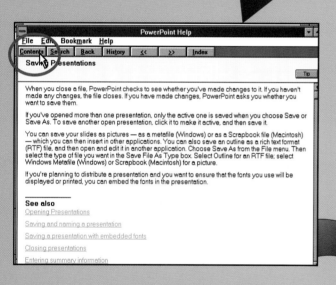

6 In the Contents page, click **Using PowerPoint** (you can click the words, or the picture of the computer). You see the Contents dialog box on the left side of the screen.

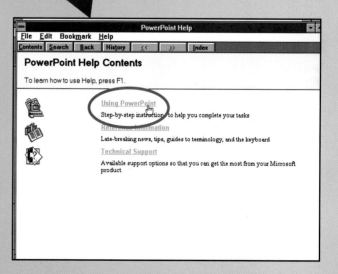

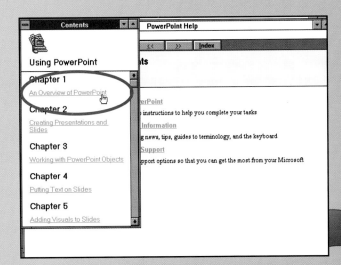

7 Click **An Overview of PowerPoint**. You see the table of contents to the first chapter of PowerPoint's manual—right on your screen!

8 Click **Overview**. You see the help page titled An Overview of PowerPoint.

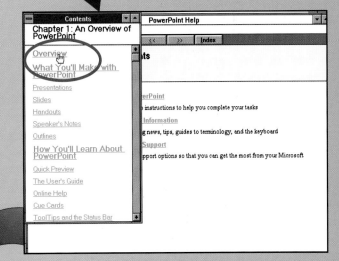

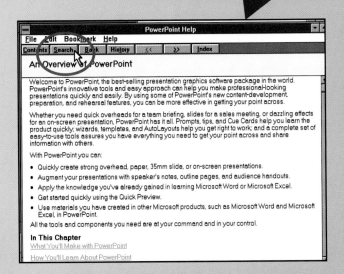

9 Here's another way to use Help. Click the **Search** button. You see the Search dialog box.

10 Type **help**. As you do, the list scrolls as it attempts to match the text you're typing.

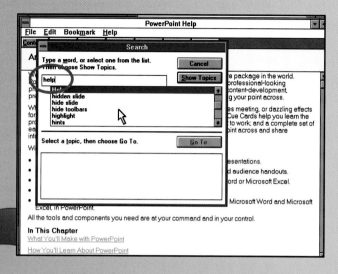

11 Click **Show Topics**. Three topics appear in the list at the bottom of the box. Double-click **Online Help**. You see an overview of everything you can do with Help. To see more of the text, click the **down arrow** on the scroll bar.

WHY WORRY?

To double-click, just click the left mouse button two times in rapid succession.

12 To close Help at any time, just double-click the **Control menu** buttons in the two Help windows. You see PowerPoint again.

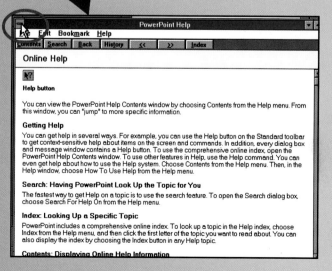

Using PowerPoint's Windows

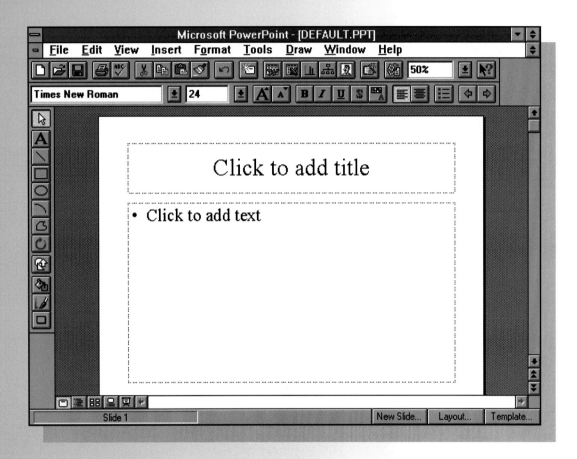

"Why would I do this?"

Like other Windows applications, PowerPoint employs the standard Windows procedures for *maximizing* windows (zooming them to full size), *restoring* a window to the previous smaller size, and *minimizing* a window down to an icon. You should know how to use the buttons that perform these actions. If you have already learned how to use these buttons, just skip to Task 4.

Task 3: Using PowerPoint's Windows

1 PowerPoint is preset to be maximized—it fills the entire screen. Try clicking the **Restore** button. This reduces Power-Point's window so that you can see other applications, including minimized icons.

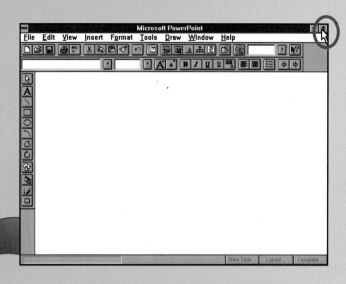

2 To zoom the screen back to full size, click the **Maximize** button. For now, however, click the **Minimize** button. This shrinks PowerPoint down to an icon. You see Program Manager, and you can now perform other tasks.

3 To see PowerPoint again, you just double-click the **PowerPoint** icon.

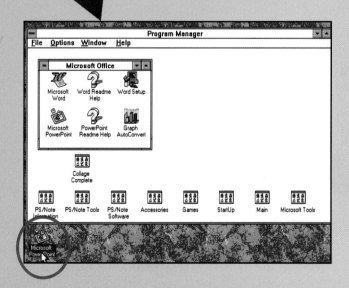

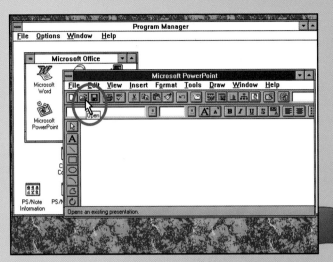

4 With PowerPoint on-screen again, click the tool on the Standard toolbar, or choose **Open** from the **File** menu. You see the Open dialog box.

5 In the **File name** drop-down list box, double-click **default.ppt**. You see the default presentation again. It appears in a *document window*. Note that this window has its own minimize and restore icons. Try them to see what they do.

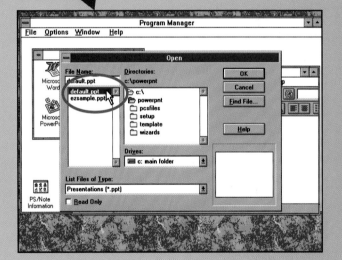

TASK 4

Using Cue Cards

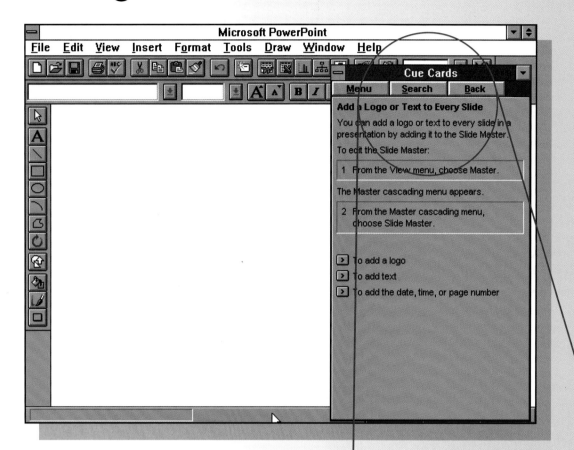

"Why would I do this?"

Cue Cards guide you through some tasks. The instructions remain on-screen while you're performing the task. You will see a Cue Card when you create your first presentation using AutoContent Wizard in Part II, "Creating a Presentation." Take a moment now to learn how to use Cue Cards.

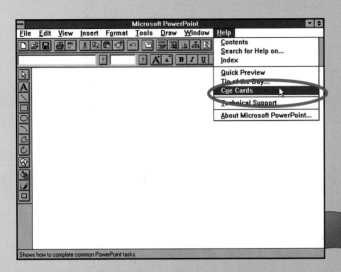

1 With PowerPoint open, choose **Cue Cards** from the **Help** menu. You see a Cue Card menu.

2 Click the button next to the first option. You see the instructions for adding a logo to every slide.

WHY WORRY?

To go back to the menu Cue Card, just click the Menu button. You can also search for Help topics by clicking Search. This works just like Search in the Help dialog box.

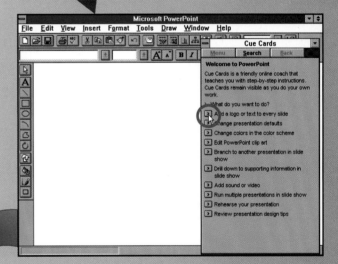

3 That's enough for now. To quit Cue Cards, just double-click the **Control menu** button.

TASK 5
Saving and Closing a Presentation

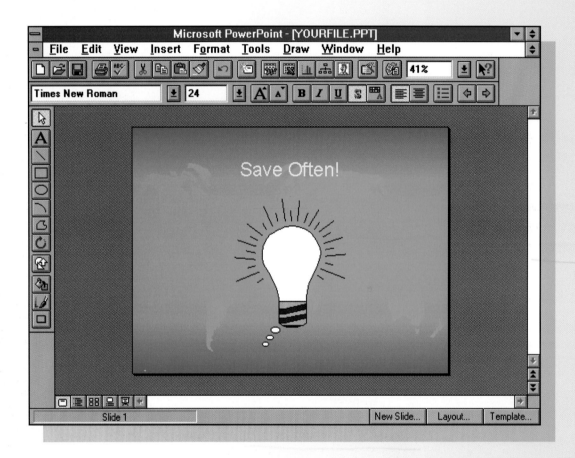

"Why would I do this?"

The work you do with PowerPoint isn't permanent until you choose the Save command. Until then, it's kept in your computer's memory; however, this memory clears when you turn off your computer. When you save your presentation, you give it a name of up to eight characters (letters or numbers). You use this name to retrieve your presentation, when you want to work on it again or produce presentation media.

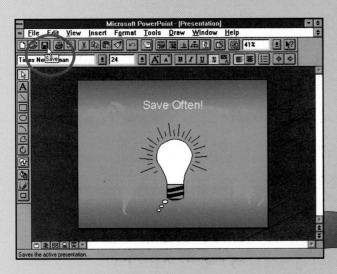

1 Click the **Save** tool on the toolbar. You also can choose **Save** from the **File** menu, or press **Ctrl+S**. You see the Save dialog box.

2 In the **File Name** text box, type a name for your file, and then click **OK** to save your work.

WHY WORRY?

If you see an alert box asking whether you want to save changes to your presentation, you made a change since the last time you saved. Just click Yes to save your presentation.

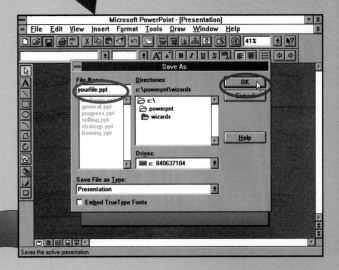

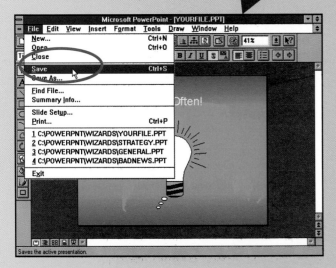

3 From here, you can close your presentation and work on another, or you can exit PowerPoint. To close your presentation, choose **Close** from the **File** menu.

NOTE ▼

The next time you save your work, you won't see the Save dialog box. PowerPoint just saves your work. To avoid losing your work due to a power outage, be sure to save your work frequently while you are working.

Opening an Existing Presentation

"Why would I do this?"

If you would like to work on your presentation after closing it, you first must reopen it to display it on-screen. You can work on any aspect of your presentation, including editing the text or changing the look.

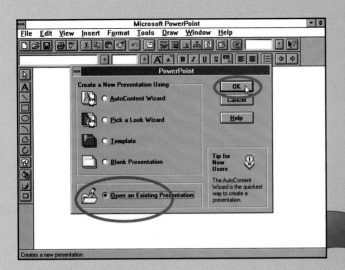

1 When you start PowerPoint, you see the PowerPoint dialog box. To open an existing presentation, click the **Open an Existing Presentation** command. Click OK. The Open dialog box appears.

2 To open the presentation you want, click the name of your presentation in the **File Name** list box, and click **OK**.

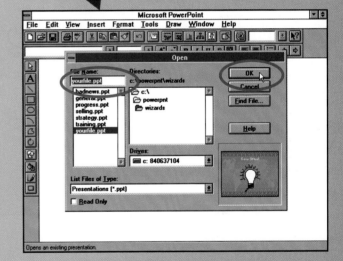

NOTE ▼

If you don't see the PowerPoint dialog box on-screen, here's a quick way to open your presentation: Just click the Open button on the toolbar. This displays the Open dialog box. If the file you want to open is one of the last four you saved, you can quickly open the file just by choosing its name from the File menu. This menu lists automatically the last four presentations you saved.

PART II
Creating a New Presentation

I n PowerPoint, you create your presentation using just one file. It contains everything you need—an outline of your presentation, your slides, audience handouts, and even your speaker's notes.

You can use PowerPoint to plan every aspect of a winning presentation. PowerPoint even helps you organize the ideas in your presentation. To get this help, use PowerPoint's AutoContent Wizard. This wizard quickly creates your presentation, including a title slide and several slides containing bulleted lists.

The wizard gives you ideas on how to organize your presentation, too. When you use the wizard, you choose from six professionally designed ways of organizing your presentation. All you need to do is type your own ideas in the place of the suggestions the wizard provides. With AutoContent wizard, you have a professional communications consultant helping you with each step!

You can choose from the following ways to organize your presentation.

■ *General*: Your presentation begins with a slide stating the topic of discussion. You continue with a slide that lists your main ideas. Next come slides that provide details on each subtopic, followed by slides that provide examples. you conclude with a summary and a statement of the next step that should be taken.

■ *Recommending a Strategy*: You begin by stating your objective in the presentation, and continue with the present situation, the desired outcome, the potential strategies, the advantages and disadvantages of your proposed strategy, and your recommendation.

■ *Selling a Product, Service, or Idea*: You start with your objective, and continue by stating the customer's requirements, the features of your product, your competetive strengths, the key benefits you can provide, and the customer's next steps.

■ *Training*: You start by stating the subject and agenda. You continue with slides that provide an overview and define your vocabulary. Next are slides for each topic you want to cover. You conclude with a summary and a list of other information sources.

■ *Reporting Progress*: You begin by providing background, and then specifying the status at present. You continue with slides

Market Share Analysis
• Exisiting Accounts
• Potential Sales
• Regional Competition
• Projected Growth

that state the accomplishments thus far, the schedule, the issues that have arisen, and your prioritization of the issues. You conclude by discussing the next phase.

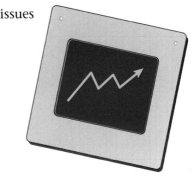

- *Communicating Bad News:* You start by providing some background on the situation. Next you consider the alternatives. You then provide a recommendation and a vision for the future. You conclude by specifying a time frame for the expected results.

AutoContent Wizard doesn't force you to follow its suggestions. After you create your presentation with this wizard, you easily can tailor it to suit your needs. You add your own text by just typing over PowerPoint's suggestions. You also can add your own slides—as many as you need to deal with your ideas.

AutoContent Wizard creates your presentation with a series of bulleted list slides. These contain lines of text preceded by a bullet (a dot). For an effective presentation, you should vary your slides by adding new *slide layouts*, including the following:

- *Clip Art:* PowerPoint comes with a library of clip art pictures. By adding one to a text slide, you create visual interest that helps you keep your audience's attention.

- *Tables:* A two-column table can help your audience grasp your material quickly. You can, for example, list your competition's services on the left—and your services on the right.

- *Graphs:* A bar chart provides quick visual cues to the trends and comparisons you want your audience to see. With PowerPoint, you can create one very easily just by typing in new numbers in place of sample data.

- *Organization Charts:* You quickly can create just the chart you need by typing in names and titles and rearranging the boxes with the mouse.

When you finish creating your slides, you can type speaker's notes and preview your presentation. You then save your presentation—your outline, slides, and notes—in just one presentation file, which you can easily open later and fine-tune the way you want.

Creating a New Presentation with AutoContent Wizard

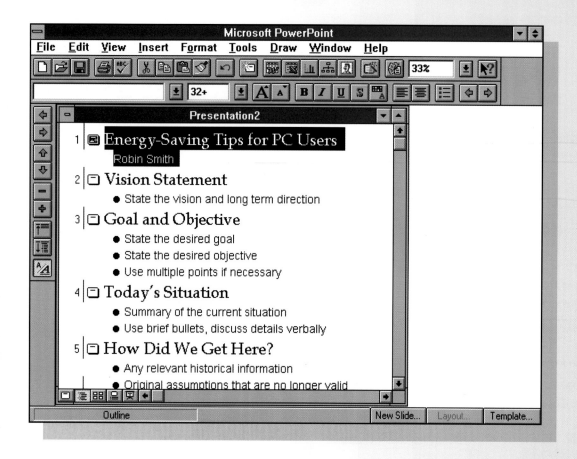

"Why would I do this?"

With PowerPoint, you could begin with a blank presentation—but leave that to the experts. Creating a blank presentation is so much easier and faster with AutoContent Wizard. It's the best way to get started with PowerPoint.

In this task, you start the wizard, choose a title for your presentation, and tell the wizard how you want to organize your data.

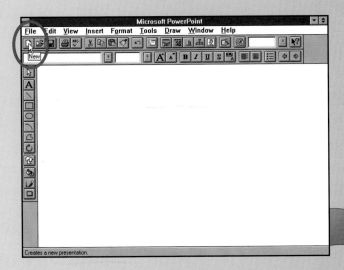

1 Click the **New** tool on the toolbar.

2 In the New Presentation dialog box, click **AutoContent Wizard** and click **OK**. The AutoContent Wizard - Step 1 of 4 dialog box appears.

WHY WORRY?

If the PowerPoint dialog box is not on-screen, just click the AutoContent Wizard tool on the toolbar.

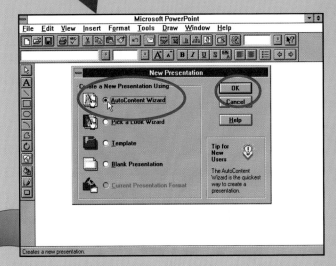

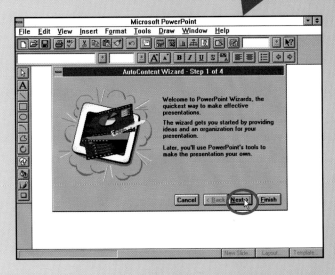

3 Click **Next>** to continue. The AutoContent Wizard - Step 2 of 4 dialog box appears.

4 Click the **What are you going to talk about?** text box and type **Energy-Saving Tips for PC Users**. PowerPoint uses this text as the title for the presentation.

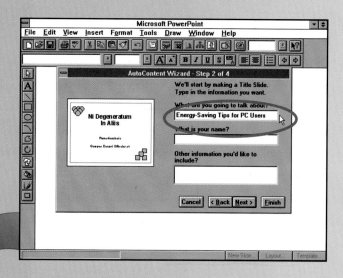

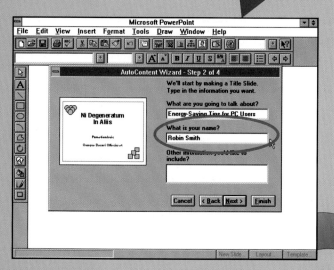

5 Press **Tab** to highlight the text in the **What is your name?** text box. Type **Robin Smith**. The text you type replaces the highlighted text in the text box.

WHY WORRY?

If you make a mistake while typing, just press Backspace to delete the error and then retype. You also can click the insertion point within the text you just typed and then press Backspace to erase the character to the left of the insertion point or press Delete to erase the character to the right of the insertion point.

6 Press **Tab** to move to the **Other information you'd like to include?** text box and type **Southwestern Power**. When you're finished, click **Next>**. The AutoContent Wizard - Step 3 of 4 dialog box appears.

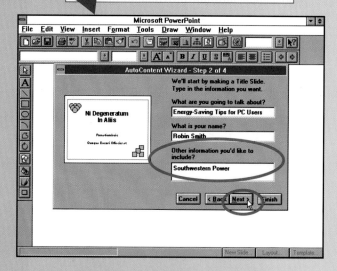

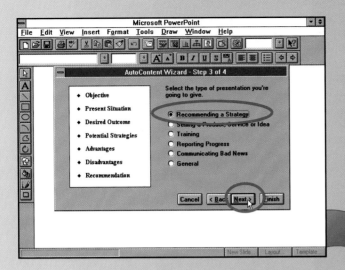

7 Click **Recommending a Strategy** to choose how you want the wizard to organize your ideas. Click **Next>** and the AutoContent Wizard - Step 4 of 4 appears.

8 To return to any of the dialog boxes, click **Back**. If your choices are correct, click **Finish**. PowerPoint creates your presentation automatically and displays an outline of your slides!

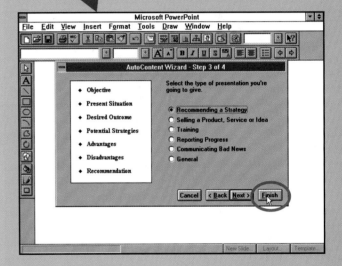

Using Outline View

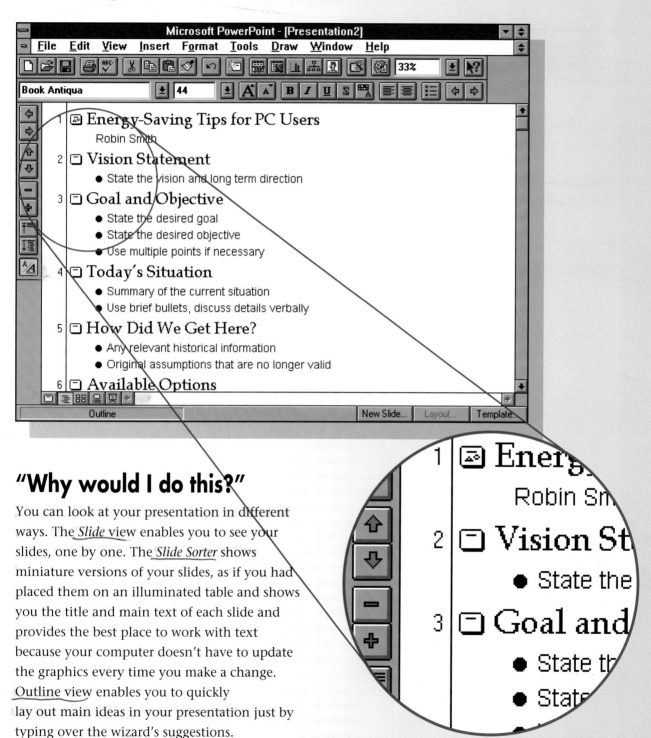

"Why would I do this?"

You can look at your presentation in different ways. The *Slide* view enables you to see your slides, one by one. The *Slide Sorter* shows miniature versions of your slides, as if you had placed them on an illuminated table and shows you the title and main text of each slide and provides the best place to work with text because your computer doesn't have to update the graphics every time you make a change. Outline view enables you to quickly lay out main ideas in your presentation just by typing over the wizard's suggestions.

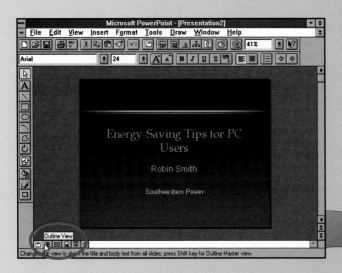

1 Click the **Outline view** button on the bottom of the window.

> **NOTE** ▼
>
> Outline view has its own toolbar. These tools help you work with your presentation.

2 Click the **Show Formatting** tool on the toolbar to use a standard font and font size in Outline view. PowerPoint shows your text using the fonts and font sizes the wizard selected for you. They look nice, but it's easier to create your presentation when you can see more text in the window.

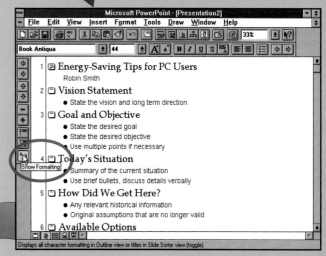

3 Click the **Show Titles** tool to see just the title for each slide. This enables you to see the overall shape of your presentation.

> **NOTE** ▼
>
> The thick gray line under the title indicates that some text is hidden.

Task 8: Using Outline View

4 Move the pointer over the slide icon following one of the numbers. When the mouse pointer changes to a four-pronged arrow, click the left mouse button. Select **Vision Statement**.

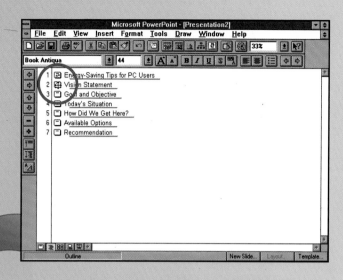

5 Click the **Expand Selection** tool on the toolbar to see the text of the selected slide.

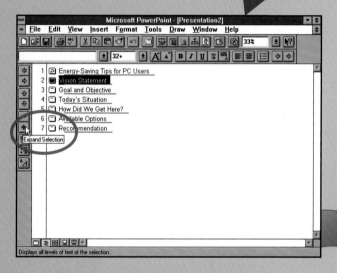

6 Click the **Collapse Selection** tool on the toolbar to hide the text in the selected slide so that just the title appears.

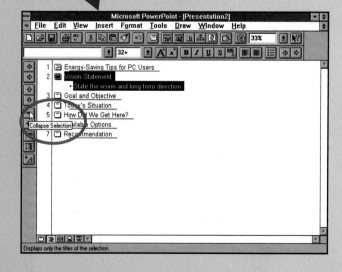

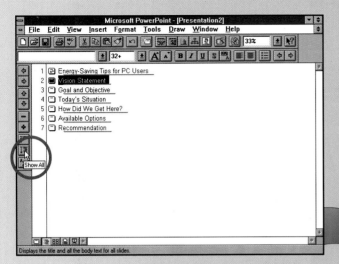

7 Click the **Show All** tool on the toolbar to see all the main text under each title.

8 Click the down scroll arrow to display the hidden portion of the outline. You also can drag down the scroll box or press **PgDn**. To scroll back up, click the up scroll arrow, drag the scroll box back up, or press **PgUp**.

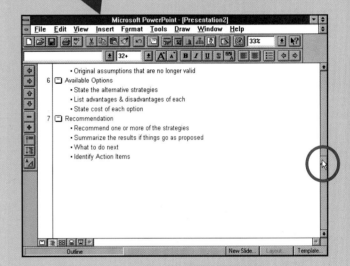

Working with Text in an Outline

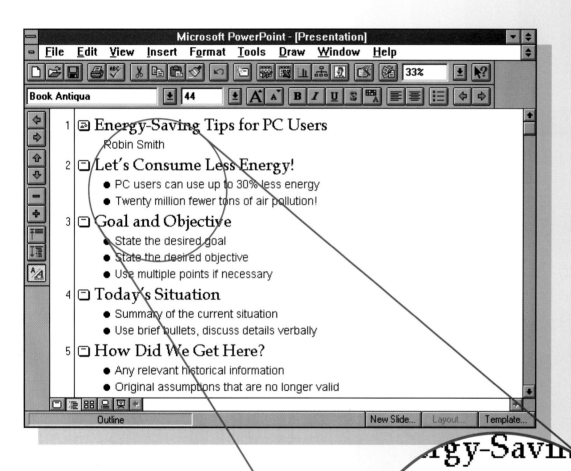

"Why would I do this?"

When you create a presentation with
AutoContent, the wizard places text on each
slide it creates. This text contains great tips for
creating a high-impact presentation. You can
change this text to express the ideas you want
to convey. In this task, you learn how to select
and change the text in Outline view. Slide 2 is
used as an example.

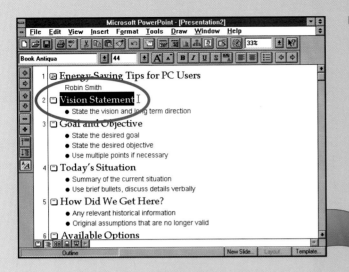

1 Select **Vision Statement** by clicking the insertion point before the word Vision and then drag the mouse to the right until both words are highlighted. Release the mouse button.

2 Type **Let's Consume Less Energy!**. As you type, the new text replaces the old text.

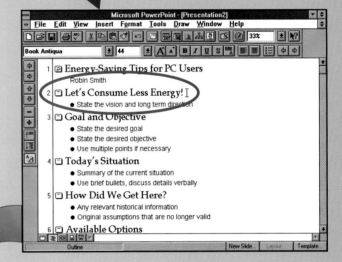

3 Select **State the vision and long term direction** by clicking and dragging (as in step 1) or click the bullet, and then type **PC users can use up to 30% less energy**.

4 Press **Enter** to start a new line. PowerPoint automatically adds a bullet to the beginning of the new line.

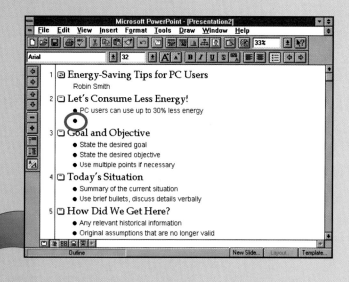

5 Type **Twenty million fewer tons of air pollution!**.

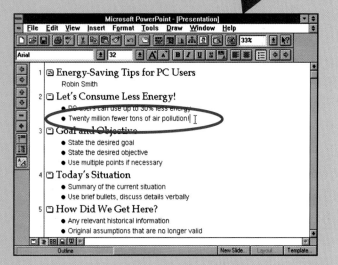

Viewing and Correcting Slides

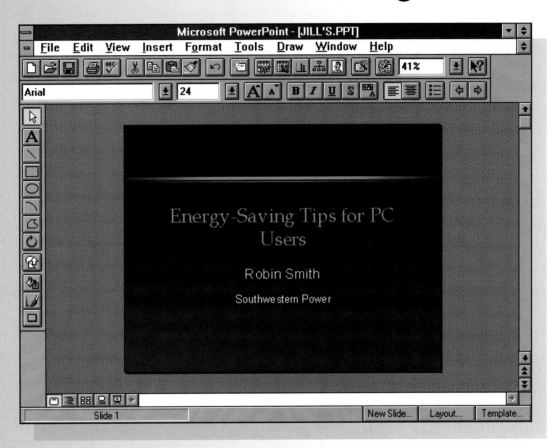

"Why would I do this?"

The Outline view gives you a convenient way to work with text. But you also need to see what your slide looks like. Perhaps you have too much text on a line in a bulleted list. Switching to the *Slide view* enables you to see how your slide will look. You also need to use Slide view for another reason. Outline view shows only the title and main text of the slide—it does not show graphics, such as clip art, graphs, or drawings. To add these enhancements, you first switch to Slide view.

43

Task 10: Viewing and Correcting Slides

1 In Outline view of the presentation you edited in Task 7, select the **Let's Consume Less Energy!** slide. When you switch to Slide view, you see the slide you have highlighted in the outline.

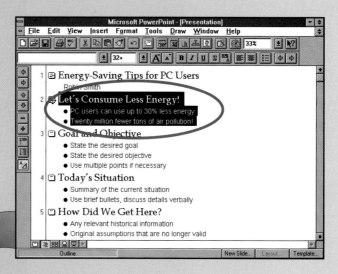

2 Click the **Slide View** tool on the toolbar at the bottom of the screen. The bulleted list slide appears. You see that the text of the first bullet does not fit on one line. Because it's best to keep bulleted items to one line, let's change it.

3 To enable text editing in Slide view, click the text you want to change. A thick bar appears around the text area.

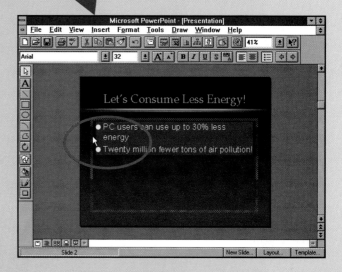

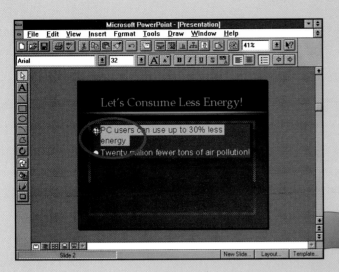

4 To select the line of text that is too long, click the bullet.

5 Type **Save 30% on your PC energy bills**. The text you type replaces the existing text.

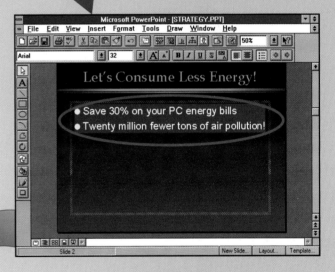

6 Click the double arrows on the scroll bar to display the previous slide, which is your title slide. To switch back to Outline view, click the **Outline View** tool on the bottom of the window.

NOTE ▼

PowerPoint updates your outline automatically to include the changes you made in Slide view.

TASK 11
Changing the Slide Layout

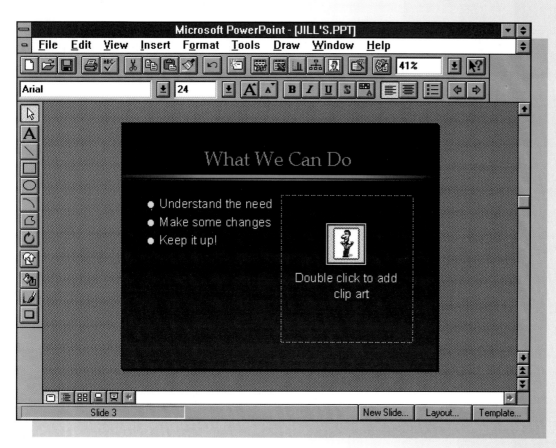

"Why would I do this?"

When the AutoContent Wizard lays out your
presentation, it creates a series of bulleted list
slides. However, one text slide after another
makes a very boring presentation. To add visual
interest to your presentation, you can vary the
layout of your slides. You can choose from 21
slide layouts (called *AutoLayouts*), including
many that enable you to add visually
interesting features, such as clip art, graphs,
organization charts, and tables. In this task, you
change the layout of Slide 3 so that you easily
can add clip art.

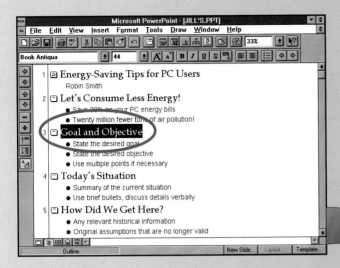

1 In Outline view of Slide 3, highlight **Goal and Objective** and type **What We Can Do**. The text you type replaces the existing text.

WHY WORRY?

If you don't see Outline view, click the Outline View tool at the bottom of the window. If the text in Slide 3 is hidden, click the Expand Selection tool on the toolbar.

2 Highlight **State the desired goal** and type **Understand the need**. Highlight **State the desired objective** and type **Make some changes**. Highlight **Use multiple points if necessary** and type **Keep it up!**.

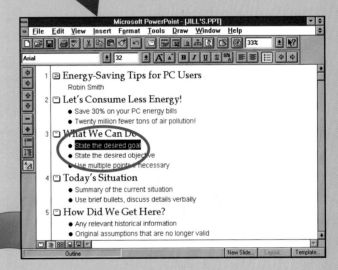

3 Click the **Slide View** tool on the status bar to switch to the Slide view. You see Slide 3, (the slide selected when you clicked the icon).

WHY WORRY?

If you see a different slide, click the Next Slide or Previous Slide tool on the scroll bar until you see Slide 3.

Task 11: Changing the Slide Layout

4 Click the **Layout** button. You find this button on the right side of the status bar, at the bottom of the screen. The Slide Layout dialog box appears.

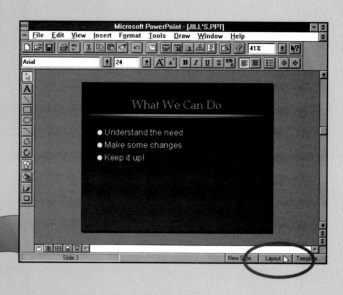

5 You see 9 of PowerPoint's 21 AutoLayouts. (To see the rest, you can click the scroll bars.) AutoLayouts contain ready-to-use placeholders for titles, text, and other features, such as graphs, clip art, and tables. A black box outlines the AutoLayout that currently is selected, while the area below the buttons shows the currently-selected AutoLayout's title.

6 Click the **Text & Clip Art** AutoLayout in the lower left corner. Click **Apply** to confirm your choice. PowerPoint changes the current slide's layout by adding an AutoLayout that contains a placeholder for clip art.

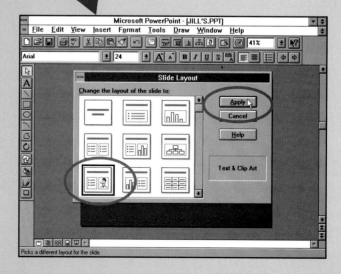

Adding Clip Art

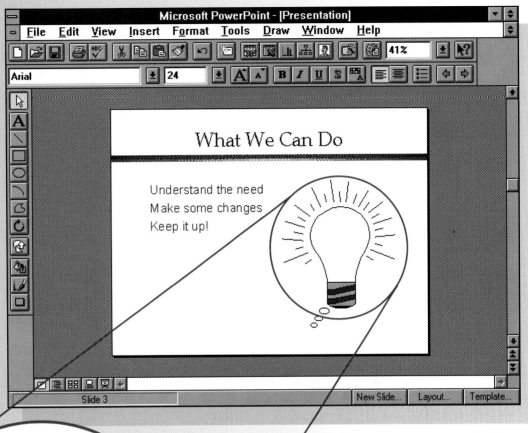

"Why would I do this?"

Clip art adds visual interest to your PowerPoint presentation. With PowerPoint's ClipArt Gallery, you can choose from more than 1,000 professionally-prepared images. Adding a clip art image is easy when you're using one of PowerPoint's AutoLayouts. You just double-click the clip art placeholder and choose the clip art you want.

Task 12: Adding Clip Art

1 In Slide view, display the slide containing the clip art placeholder, if it isn't already on-screen. Double-click the placeholder.

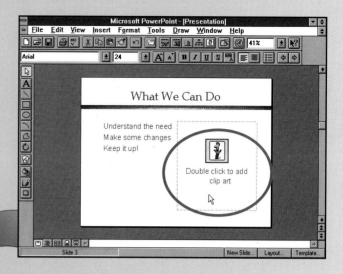

2 PowerPoint displays the Microsoft ClipArt Gallery - Picture in Presentation dialog box. In the list box titled `Choose a category to view below`, click the down scroll arrow until you see the Clip Art Gallery of your choice, and then click it.

WHY WORRY?

If you're using clip art for the first time, you may see a dialog box asking whether you would like to add the clip art images to PowerPoint now. Click OK. This may take a few minutes.

3 In the area that shows the clip art images, click the down scroll arrow until you see the image you want, and then click it. Click **OK** to add the artwork to your presentation!

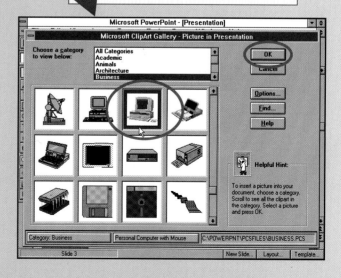

TASK 13

Deleting an AutoLayout

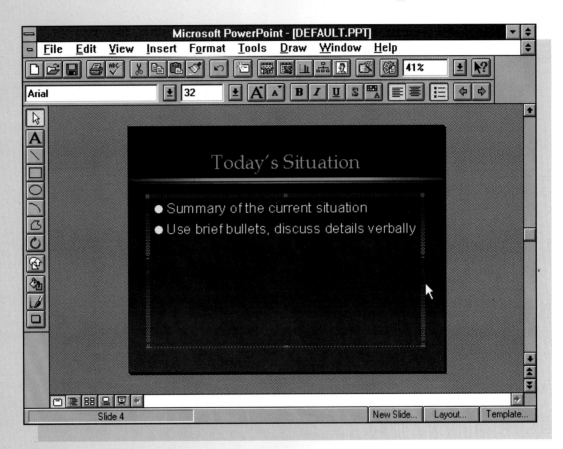

"Why would I do this?"

To vary your presentation visually, you should create slides that contain more visually interesting material (and no bulleted lists). To do so, you want to choose slide layouts that contain placeholders for tables, graphs, drawings, and organization charts. But first you delete the bulleted list placeholder.

Task 13: Deleting an AutoLayout

1 In Slide view, display the slide that contains the bulleted list AutoLayout that you want to delete. For this example, you will delete the bulleted list in Slide 4, `Today's Situation`.

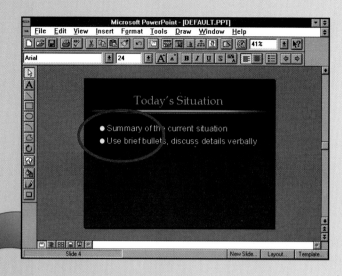

2 Click anywhere within the bulleted list. You see a thick border around the bulleted list placeholder.

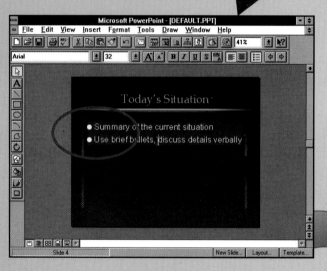

3 Click the thick border. You see eight square boxes on the border now. These are the resizing handles. You can use these to change the size of the objects you place on PowerPoint slides, as discussed in Part III.

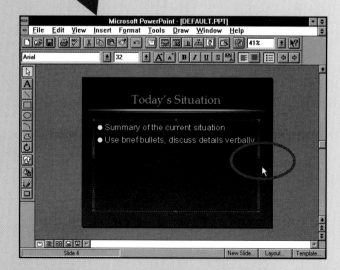

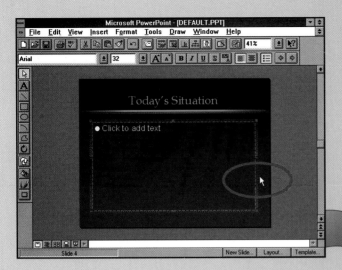

4 Press **Delete**. This deletes the text that AutoContent Wizard inserted. You see the bulleted list placeholder.

WHY WORRY?

If you can't get the resizing handles to appear, you may not be pointing and clicking correctly. Point with the *tip* of the arrow.

5 Press **Delete** again to delete the bulleted list placeholder. Now the area below the title is blank. You now can change to an AutoLayout that takes up this entire area.

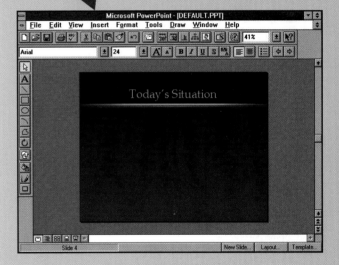

TASK 14

Creating a Table

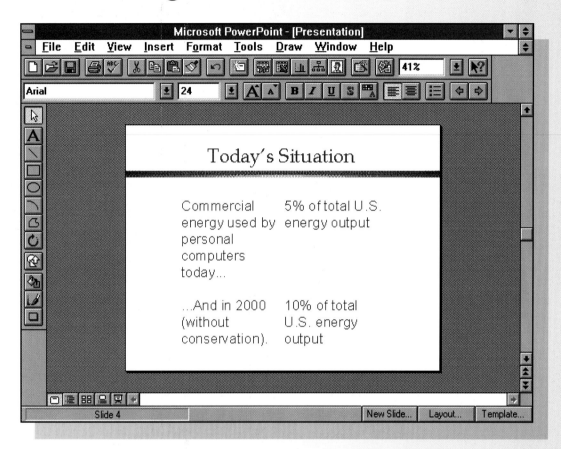

"Why would I do this?"

A table provides a great way to list items and show relationships. For presentations, use no more than two or three columns and three or four rows. If you need to show patterns in more complex data, use a graph. In PowerPoint, tables can contain figures or words, or both. After you create a table, you just click within a table box and type. PowerPoint automatically adjusts the size of the box to accommodate what you type. For this example, you will need to display Slide 4 on-screen.

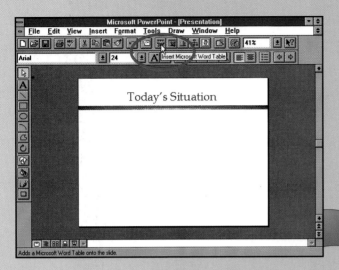

1 Click the **Insert Microsoft Word Table** tool on the toolbar. You see a table layout pad. This enables you to choose the number of rows and columns you want.

NOTE ▼

You must have Word 6 for Windows to use the Table function.

2 Move the pointer to the box in the upper left corner of the table layout pad, and drag right and down until you have selected two rows and two columns. You see `2 x 2 Table` at the bottom of the table layout pad.

WHY WORRY?

If you created the wrong number of columns or rows, just click anywhere on the slide background to close the table. Press Delete to remove the table, and repeat steps 1 and 2.

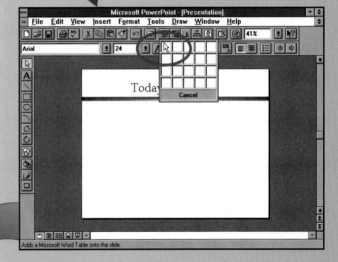

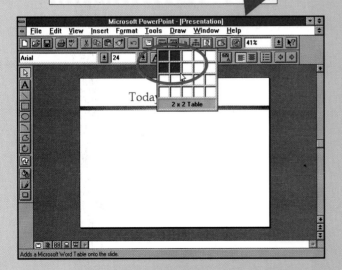

3 Release the mouse button. PowerPoint creates and opens the table in a special window. The table has four boxes, called *cells*, which are formed by the dotted lines. Click the top left cell, and type **Commercial energy used by personal computers today....** Press **Enter** to leave a blank line under this.

Task 14: Creating a Table

4 Click in the bottom left cell, and type **...And in 2000 (without conservation).**

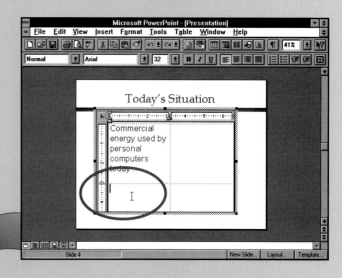

5 Click the top right cell, and type **5% of total U.S. energy output.**

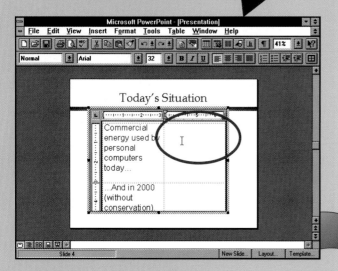

WHY WORRY?

Should you need to edit the table to correct a mistake, just double-click within the table area. You will see the table window again, and you can make the changes you want. Just click the slide background to close the table.

6 Click the bottom right cell, and type **10% of total U.S. energy output**. You're done! To close the table window, just click on the slide background.

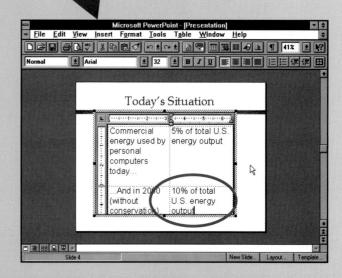

TASK 15
Creating a Graph

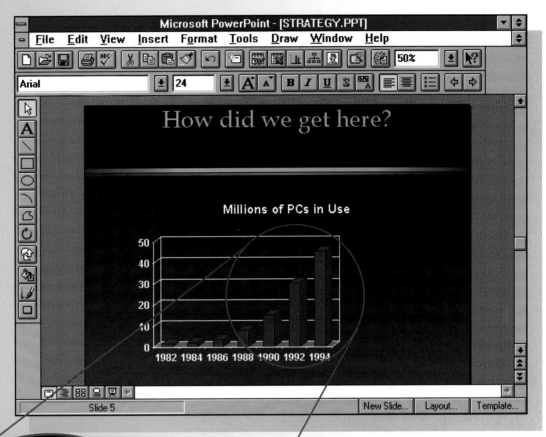

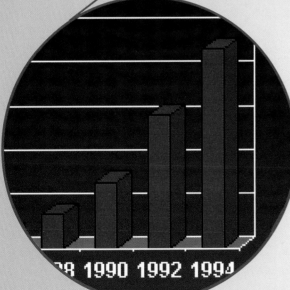

"Why would I do this?"

A table provides a handy way to summarize a few facts and figures. To show trends and comparisons in more complex data, however, it is better to use a graph. For this example, you must be in Slide view with Slide 5, How Did We Get Here?, on-screen.

Task 15: Creating a Graph

1 Click the bulleted list text area until you see the thick border. Click this border to display the selection handles.

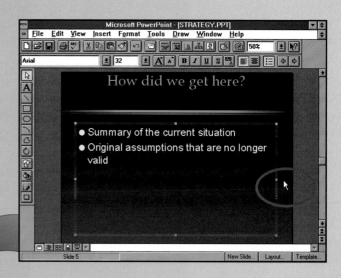

2 Press **Delete** twice. This removes this text object and the bulleted list AutoLayout. Click the **Layout** button. The Slide Layout dialog box appears.

3 Click **Graph**. The name of the chart appears in the area in the lower right corner of the Slide Layout dialog box. This is the chart on the upper right corner. Click **Apply** to change the slide to this layout. You see a Graph placeholder.

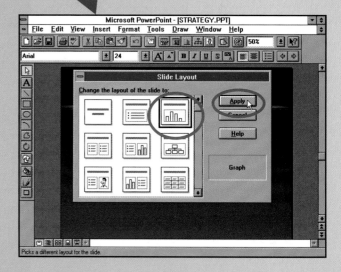

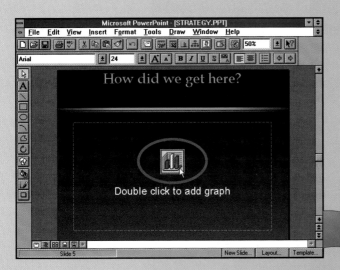

4 Double-click the icon in the center of the screen. PowerPoint starts Microsoft Graph, and after a few moments, you see a datasheet. In the background, you see a chart on your slide.

WHY WORRY?

You don't have to use the data and the graph that Microsoft Graph has inserted. Graph provides them to give you something to work with. Also, by making changes to this data, you can see how Graph works.

5 In the datasheet, click the **Row 2** button—it's the one with the 2 on it.

6 Press and hold down **Shift**, and click the **Row 3** button. This selects two rows of data that you don't need for your graph. Press **Delete** to delete the text in Rows 2 and 3.

Task 15: Creating a Graph

7 Click on the datasheet's title bar and drag the datasheet window right and up so that you can see the chart beneath. Select the text **1st Qtr** (just below A), and type **1982**. The text you type replaces the existing text. Press **Tab** to select **2nd Qtr**, and type **1984**. Press **Tab** again, and type **1986**. Pressing **Tab** before each date, type **1988**, **1990**, **1992**, and **1994**.

NOTE ▼
Microsoft Graph has added the dates at the bottom of the graph.

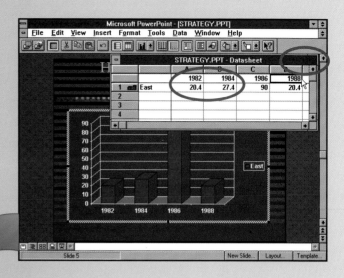

8 In the datasheet window, click the left scroll arrow until you see the row number buttons again. Double-click the word **East** in Row 1, and type **Millions of PCs in Use**.

WHY WORRY?
After you move to the next cell, you don't see all the text you just typed because of the limited display area. If you want to be sure, select the cell that contains the data.

9 Press **Tab** to highlight the second cell in Row 1 (the cell in Column A), and type **1.5**.

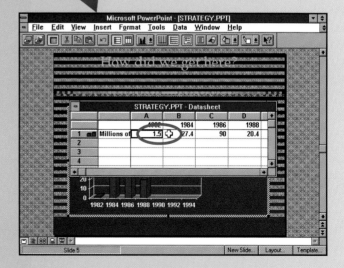

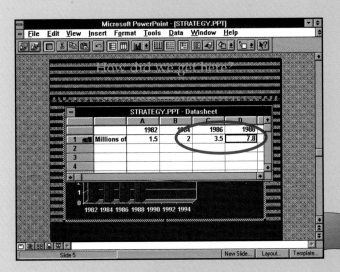

10 Press **Tab** to highlight the cell in Row 1 under Column B, and type **2.0**. Continue adding the following data, pressing **Tab** before each number: **3.5** (in Column C), **7.8** (in Column D), **15.1** (in Column E), and **30.4** (in Column F). Press **Tab** once more, and type **45.5** in Column G. Press **Enter** to confirm this last entry.

NOTE ▼

Take a look at your graph! You see bars representing data for each of the dates you have entered.

11 Click the **Datasheet** tool on the toolbar to close the Datasheet window. Now you can see your graph.

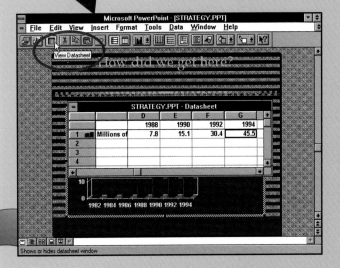

12 From the **Insert** menu, choose **Titles**. You see the Titles dialog box.

WHY WORRY?

If you don't see a Titles option in the Insert menu, you probably clicked the slide background. This closes Microsoft Graph. To open Microsoft Graph again, just double-click within the graph area.

Task 15: Creating a Graph

13 In the Titles dialog box, click **Chart Title**, and then click **OK**. In your graph, you see a text box that echoes the text you typed at the beginning of Row 1.

14 Because the legend is no longer necessary (it duplicates the title), click the **Legend** tool to hide the legend box.

15 Now select the graph area. When the resize handles appear, drag the right border resize handle to the right. To complete your graph and return to PowerPoint, just click the slide background. Congratulations!

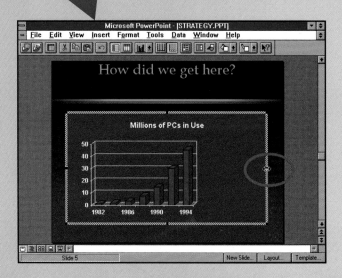

Adding an AutoShape

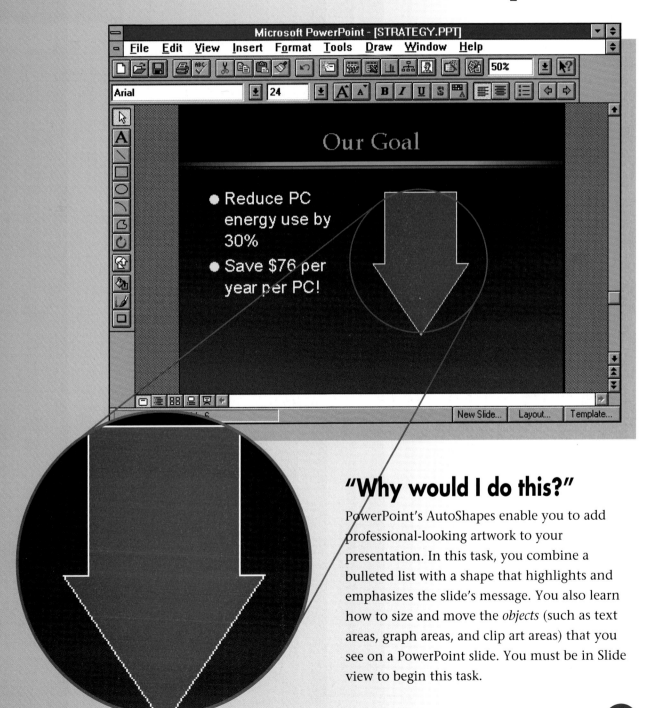

"Why would I do this?"

PowerPoint's AutoShapes enable you to add professional-looking artwork to your presentation. In this task, you combine a bulleted list with a shape that highlights and emphasizes the slide's message. You also learn how to size and move the *objects* (such as text areas, graph areas, and clip art areas) that you see on a PowerPoint slide. You must be in Slide view to begin this task.

Task 16: Adding an AutoShape

1 In Slide view, display the slide to which you want to add the artwork. This task uses Slide 6, `Available Options`, for an example.

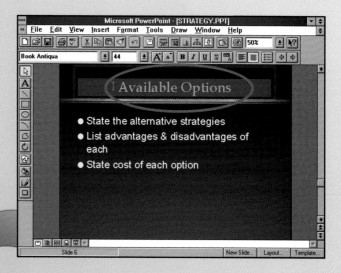

2 Select the title text and then type **Our Goal**.Click the first bullet in the bulleted list to select the text and then type **Reduce PC energy use by 30%**. Click the second bullet in the bulleted list to select the text and then type **Save $76 per year per PC!**. Click the third bullet and press **Delete**.

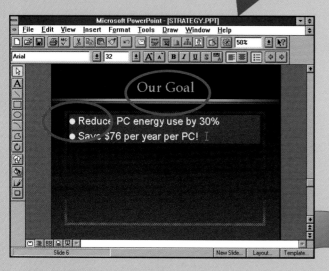

3 Let's make this list a little smaller. Click the text object border until you see the eight square resizing handles. Move the pointer to the handle in the middle of the right border, so that you see an arrow that points right and left. Click and hold down the left mouse button and drag left to shrink the object's border, until it takes up just half of the slide. PowerPoint reformats the text to fit in the reduced area.

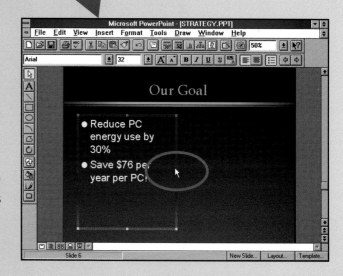

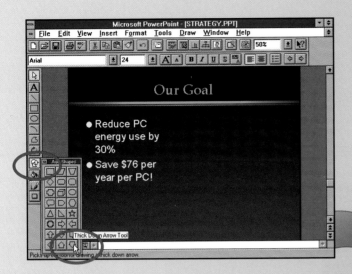

4 Now let's add the AutoShape. On the Drawing toolbar, click the **AutoShapes** tool. You see a pop-up menu of shapes from which you can choose. In the palette of AutoShape, click the **Thick Down Arrow** tool (the bottom right tool). You see a plus shape.

5 Move the pointer to the top left of the blank area on the slide. Then click and drag right and down to make the arrow. Release the mouse button.

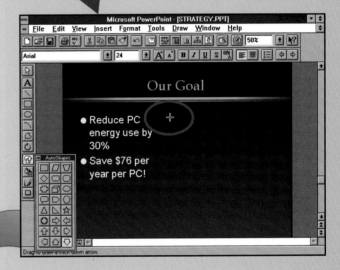

6 Double-click the AutoShape palette's **Control menu** button (the hyphen in the top left corner) to close the palette.

Adding a New Slide

"Why would I do this?"

As your presentation develops, you probably
will want to add slides to those already created
by the AutoContent Wizard. PowerPoint makes
it easy to do this! To perform this task, you
need to be in Slide view.

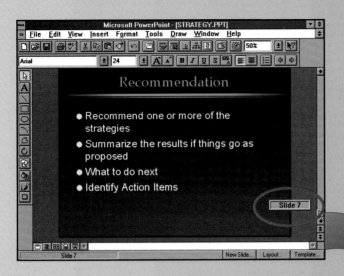

1 In Slide view, select the slide you want appear *before* the new slide. This task uses Slide 7, Available Options for an example. The new slide will become Slide 7, and the Available Options slide will become Slide 8.

NOTE ▼

You must insert your new slide in Slide view, not Outline view. Only when you insert the new slide in Slide view can you choose an AutoLayout at the same time.

2 Click the **New Slide** button at the bottom right of the screen. You see the New Slide dialog box, which enables you to choose the AutoLayout you want for your new slide.

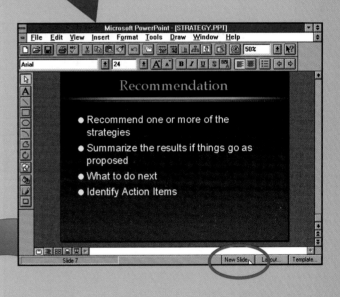

3 Click the **AutoLayout** you want. For this example, you can choose an organization chart (Org Chart). Click **OK** to confirm your choice and create the slide.

Creating an Organization Chart

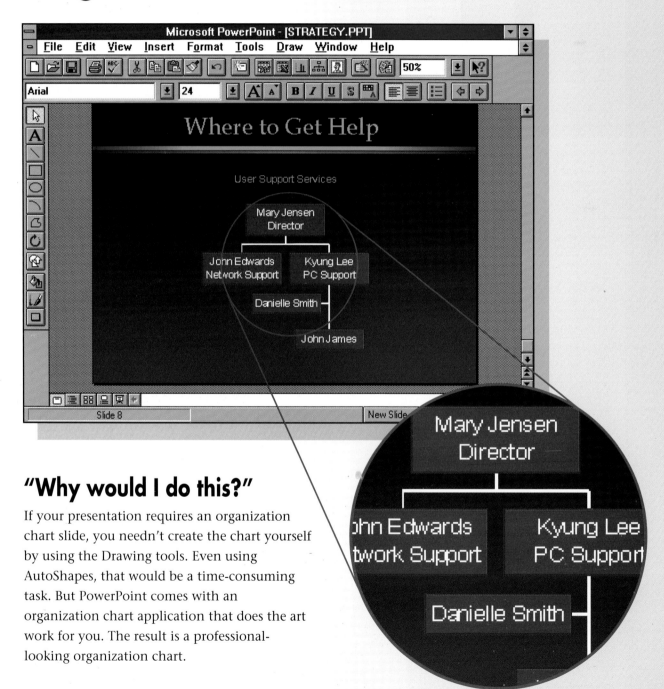

"Why would I do this?"

If your presentation requires an organization chart slide, you needn't create the chart yourself by using the Drawing tools. Even using AutoShapes, that would be a time-consuming task. But PowerPoint comes with an organization chart application that does the art work for you. The result is a professional-looking organization chart.

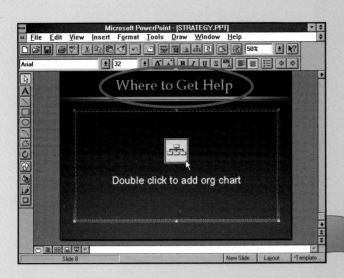

1 Display the slide to which you want to add the organization chart. This task uses the slide you created in Task 17 as an example. Highlight the title text (**Click to add title**), type **Where To Get Help**, and then double-click the icon in the center of the slide.

2 You see the Microsoft Organization Chart window. In this window, you create your organization chart by modifying the one you see. In the chart title area, click and drag to select the text, and type **User Support Services**.

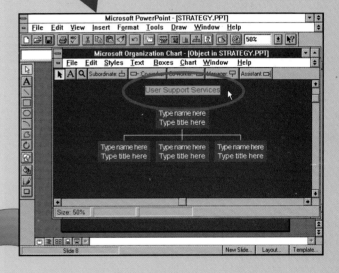

3 Click in the far right box until the box turns dark.

Task 18: Creating an Organization Chart

4 Type **Mary Jensen**, and press **Tab**. Then type **Director**.

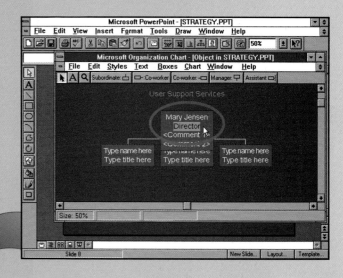

5 Now click the first of the three boxes under Mary Jensen, and type **John Edwards**. Press **Tab**, and type **Network Support**.

6 You can delete any box you don't want. Click the middle box under Mary Jensen, and press **Delete**. The middle box disappears.

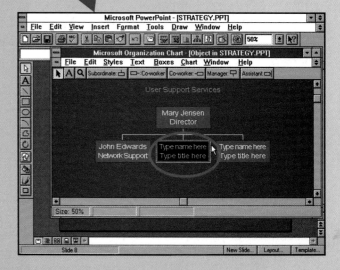

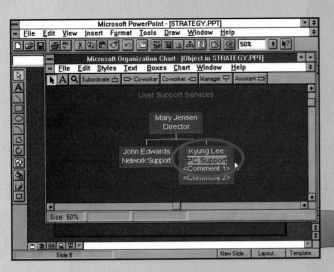

7 Now click the last blank box, and type **Kyung Lee**. Press **Tab** and type **PC Support**.

8 To add boxes to the chart, you click one of the buttons above the chart (Subordinate, Co-worker, Manager, or Assistant), and click the box where you want to add a person. Let's give Kyung an assistant. Click **Assistant**, and then click **Kyung's** box. You see a new, blank Assistant box. It's selected and ready for you to type the person's name. Type **Danielle Smith**.

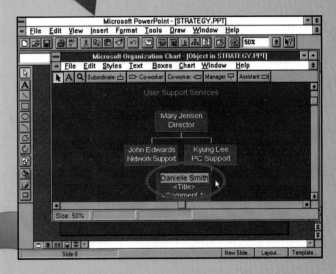

9 Now let's give Kyung a subordinate. Click the **Subordinate** button and then click Kyung Lee's box. A subordinate box appears. Type **John James** in this box. Your organization chart is done!

Task 18: Creating an Organization Chart

10 Choose **Update Presentation** from the **File** menu. The file and changes you made are updated.

NOTE ▼

If you have saved your file, this command name will include the name you gave your file. If you haven't yet named your file, the File menu says `Update Presentation`.

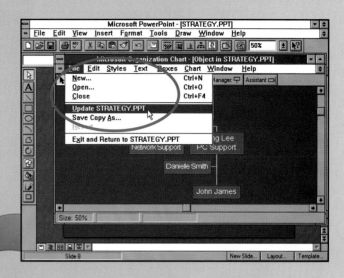

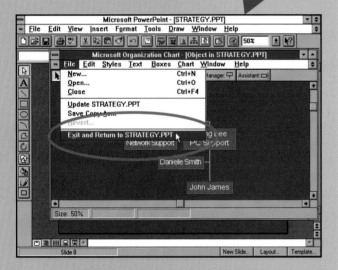

11 Now exit Organization Chart. Choose **Exit and Return** from the **File** menu. You also can exit by pressing **Alt+F4** or double-clicking the **Control menu** box (the long hyphen in the upper left corner of the window). You see your completed organization chart on your slide.

WHY WORRY?

If you see an alert box informing you that you have changed the object, you probably forgot to choose the Update command before exiting Organization Chart. Just click Yes to update your presentation with the chart you have made.

Adding Speaker's Notes

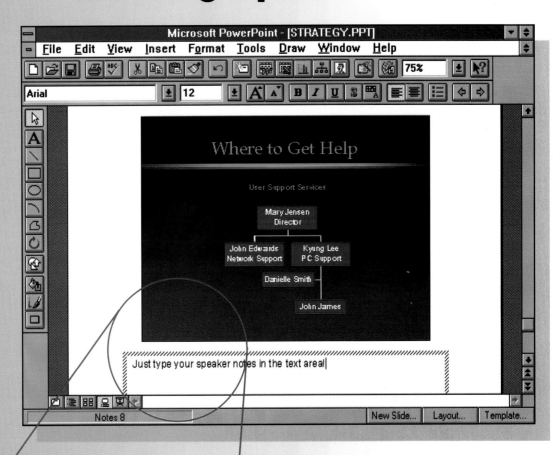

"Why would I do this?"

PowerPoint gives you room to type notes that
you can take with you to the podium. When
you print these notes, PowerPoint reproduces
the slide at the top of the page and prints your
notes at the bottom. This isn't necessary for
your presentation. If you prefer, you can place
your notes on 3 x 5 cards or paper; however,
consider using PowerPoint to make your notes
right after you create each slide when the
decisions you made when you created the slide
are still fresh in your mind. For this task, Slide 8
created in Tasks 17 and 18 is used. you can add
speaker notes to any slide, however.

Task 19: Adding Speaker's Notes

1 In Slide view, display the slide to which you want to add notes, and choose **Note Pages** from the **View menu**. You see what your note pages will look like when PowerPoint prints them—the slide is reproduced on the top of the screen, with space for your notes on the bottom.

2 Click the **Zoom Control** tool on the toolbar. When the list of zoom percentages appears, choose **100%**. This magnifies the screen so that you can see what you're writing.

WHY WORRY?

Need to make a change to your notes? No problem! Just redisplay the slide to which you have added the notes, and choose Notes Pages from the View menu.

3 Click the document window's scroll down arrow on the scroll bar so that you can see an entire line of text at a time. Click within the notes area, and type your notes. When you're finished, just click the **Slide view** icon to hide your notes.

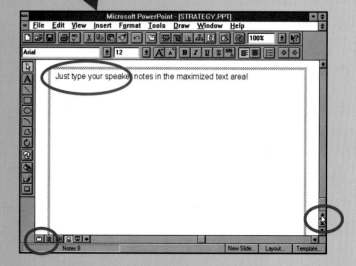

Using the Pick a Look Wizard

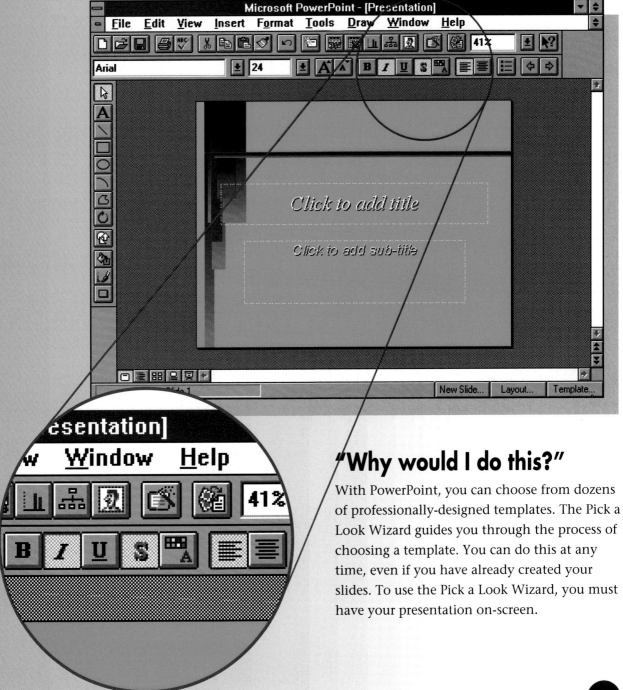

"Why would I do this?"

With PowerPoint, you can choose from dozens of professionally-designed templates. The Pick a Look Wizard guides you through the process of choosing a template. You can do this at any time, even if you have already created your slides. To use the Pick a Look Wizard, you must have your presentation on-screen.

Task 20: Using the Pick a Look Wizard

1 Click the **Pick a Look** tool on the toolbar. You see the Pick a Look Wizard - Step 1 of 9 dialog box.

WHY WORRY?

If nothing happens when you click the Pick a Look tool, you haven't opened your presentation yet. Open your presentation, and click the tool again.

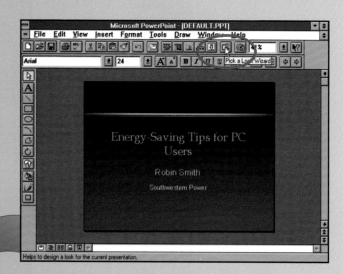

2 Click **Next >** to see the Step 2 of 9 dialog box.

NOTE ▼

If you want to use the Pick a Look Wizard starting from scratch, choose New from the File menu, click Pick a Look Wizard, click OK, and then follow along with the following steps.

3 Click the output medium you want to use. This task uses On-Screen Presentation. Click **Next >** to see the Pick a Look Wizard - Step 3 of 9 dialog box.

WHY WORRY?

If you're not yet sure which type of output to use, just leave the setting at On-Screen Presentation. You easily can change this setting later by clicking the Pick a Look tool on the toolbar and repeating these steps.

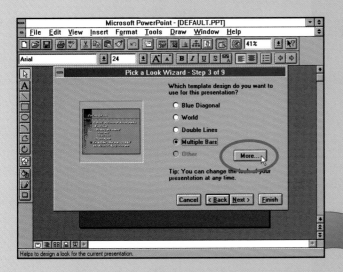

4 Here, you can click Blue Diagonal, World, Double Lines, or Multiple Bars. If you click one of these, skip to step 6 in these instructions. To choose from additional templates, click **More**. The Presentation Template dialog box appears.

NOTE ▼

In the Presentation Template dialog box, you see the templates for the type of presentation you selected. To see a different template, choose Cancel, and then click Back until you see Step 2 of 9.

5 To see a thumbnail sketch of what a template looks like, click the name in the **File Name** list box and look in the area under the Help button. If you want to see more template names, click the down scroll arrow of the File Name list box. When you have found and displayed the template you want, click **Apply**. The Pick a Look Wizard - Step 3 of 9 dialog box reappears with a thumbnail sketch of the design you chose in the area on the left of the dialog box.

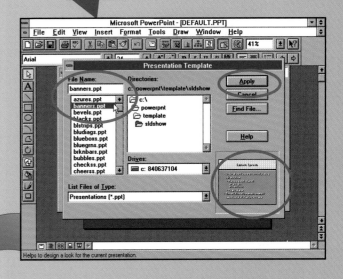

6 Click **Next >**. You see the Pick a Look Wizard - Step 4 of 9 dialog box. Here, you select the ways you want to print your presentation.

Task 20: Using the Pick a Look Wizard

7 Select or disable the printing choices you want. If you don't want to print speaker's notes, audience handouts, or outlines, deselect these options by clicking the check box to remove the X. Then PowerPoint won't ask you to choose printing options for them. If you click the **Full-Page Slides** option, PowerPoint displays the Pick a Look Wizard - Slide Options dialog box.

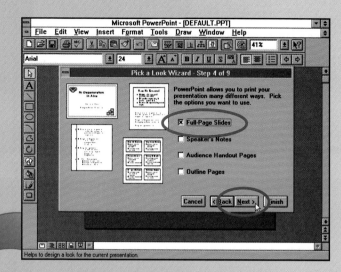

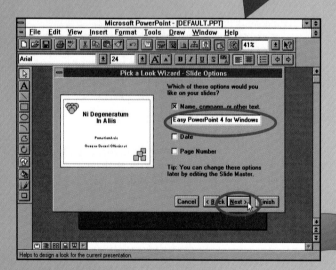

8 The Slide Options dialog box enables you to add text such as a company name, date, and slide number to your slides. If you do not want these, click the check box so that the X disappears. If you want PowerPoint to print certain text on each page, type the text in the text box. When finished with this dialog box, choose **Next >**. The Notes Options dialog box appears.

9 Choose the printing options you want for speaker's notes. You can choose to print the Name (company or other text), Date, and Page Number. After you choose your options, click **Next >**. The Handouts Options dialog box appears.

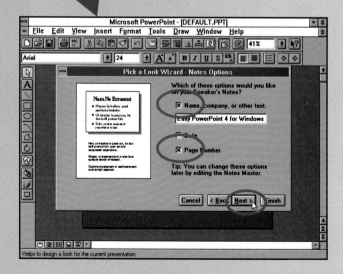

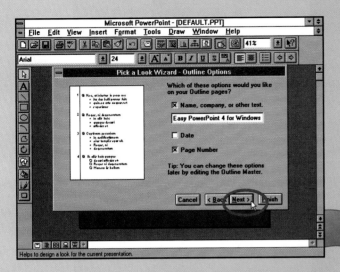

10 Choose the printing options you want for audience handouts and then click **Next >**. The Pick a Look Wizard - Outline Options dialog box appears.

11 Choose the printing options you want for outlines and then click **Next >**. The Pick a Look Wizard - Step 9 of 9 dialog box appears.

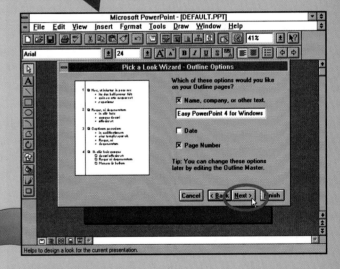

12 Click **Finish** and you're done!

WHY WORRY?

Not happy with the look? Use the Pick a Look Wizard again to choose another template. Only, don't go through all those printing options again. After choosing your template, click the Finish button to close the wizard.

PART III
Working with Objects

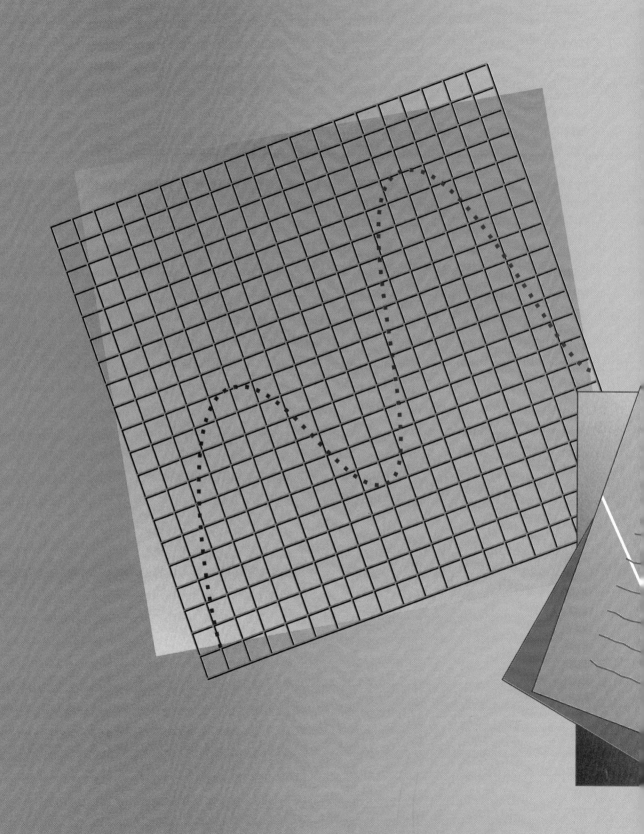

When you add features such as an AutoShape, a graph, a clip art picture, or an organization chart to your slide, you create an *object*. An object simply is a rectangular area of your slide set aside for the type of material it contains such as a table, picture, or text.

All objects share in common certain features. You can select them independently of other objects on-screen. You can duplicate them, if you want an exact copy of an object you've just created. You can resize and move objects, positioning them just where you want them. You can group them so that two or more objects move together. And you can enhance them by changing the object's *attributes*, such as line type, fill color, shadow, and embossing effect.

You can "stack" objects as if they were layered on your slide like pieces of paper in a pile on your desk so that most recent object you've worked with is on top. Sometimes you need to send objects backward, or bring others forward, so that you can see all the features you've added.

The tasks in Part III explore the basics of working with objects. You will find these skills useful. But remember that every PowerPoint template comes with default settings for objects and their attributes, including fonts for text objects. PowerPoint's designers chose these attributes because they work well with the template's distinctive style. You should enhance objects sparingly, and only when you have a good reason. You may, for example, want to add emphasis to a table by enclosing it in a box or adding a shadow effect.

TASK 21

Selecting and Grouping Objects

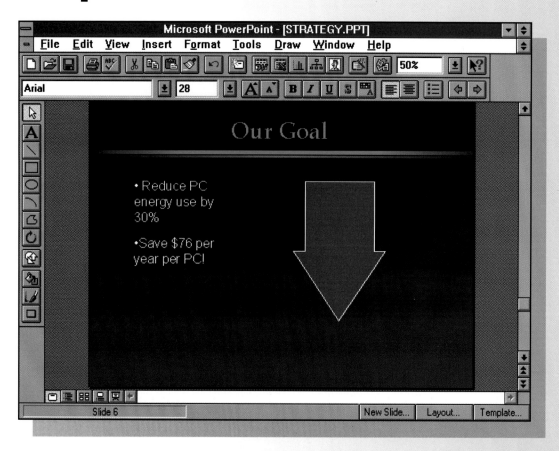

"Why would I do this?"

To manipulate a PowerPoint object, you first must select it. You then can perform actions on the object, such as moving, sizing, or enhancing it. You sometimes might want to perform an action, such as adding borders, to more than one object at a time. This saves time because you can choose the action just once, and it affects all the selected objects. The example for this task is the Slide 6, which was creating in Task 16.

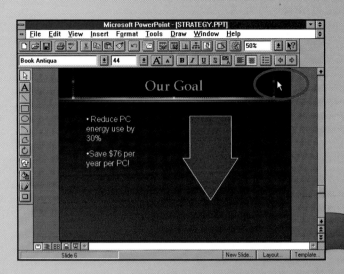

1 In Slide view, display Slide 6. Click the title and then click the border that appears. When it is selected, you see the resizing handles on the thick border that surrounds the title.

NOTE ▼

If the object you are trying to select contains the same fill color as the slide background, you must click the object's border to see the resizing handles.

2 To select a second object, press and hold down **Shift** and click the large arrow. The borders disappear and square placeholders appear.

NOTE ▼

To group selected objects quickly, point to the objects and click the right mouse button. From the pop-up menu that appears, choose Group.

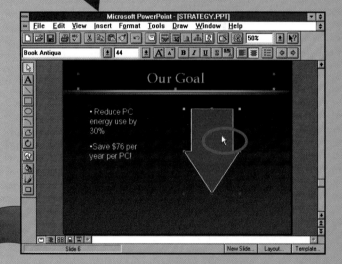

3 To group the two objects you selected, choose **Group** from the **Draw** menu. When objects are grouped, you can move them or resize them with just one mouse maneuver. The two objects now are grouped together into one object. Note that there is just one set of resize handles for both objects.

Task 21: Selecting and Grouping Objects

4 You also can ungroup objects. Try this now. Select the object and choose **Ungroup** from the **Draw** menu. Each object has its own selection handles.

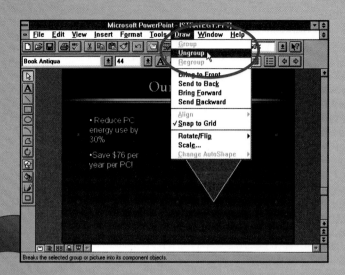

NOTE ▼

To ungroup selected objects quickly, point to the objects and click the right mouse button. From the pop-up menu that appears, choose Ungroup.

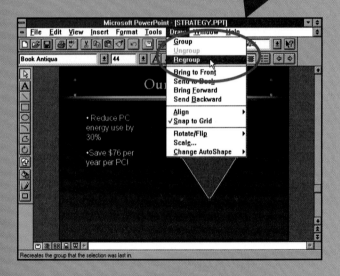

5 After you ungroup grouped objects, you don't need to select them again using Shift+Click if you want to regroup them. Just select one of the objects, and choose **Regroup** from the **Draw** menu. The objects again are grouped.

NOTE ▼

To regroup selected objects quickly, point to the objects and click the right mouse button. From the pop-up menu that appears, choose Regroup.

WHY WORRY?

To deselect an object, simply select another object or click the slide background.

Deleting Objects

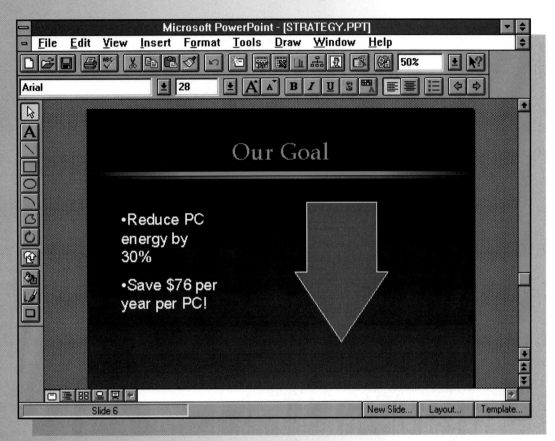

"Why would I do this?"

If you have inserted an object that you don't want to keep, or if your slide has an AutoLayout you don't want, you can delete the object. Because grouped objects act as a single object, you also can select and delete grouped objects. In addition to selecting a single object or grouped objects, you can select and delete multiple objects using the Shift+Click method described in step 5 of Task 21. This task uses Slide 6, which was created in Task 16.

Task 22: Deleting Objects

1 Click the arrow to select it.

2 Choose the **Clear** command from the **Edit** menu or press **Delete**. The object disappears.

> **WHY WORRY?**
>
> If you just deleted an object by mistake, immediately click the Undo tool on the toolbar, choose Undo from the Edit menu, or press Ctrl+Z.

Copying, Pasting, and Duplicating Objects

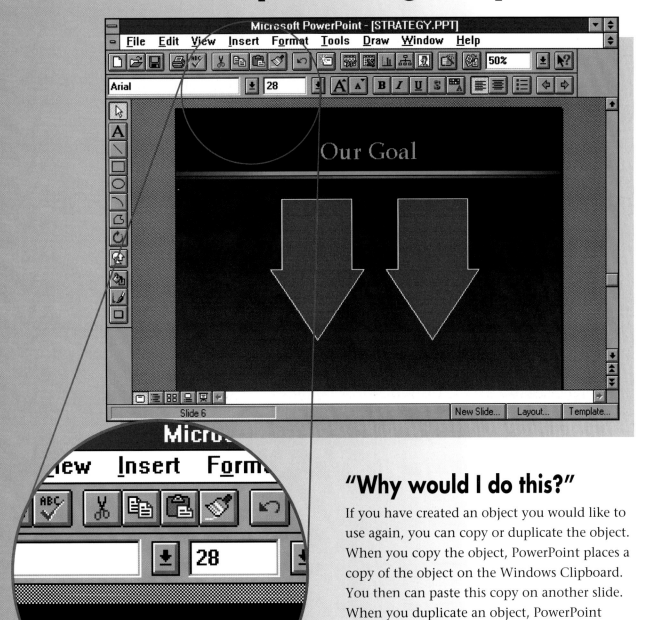

"Why would I do this?"

If you have created an object you would like to use again, you can copy or duplicate the object. When you copy the object, PowerPoint places a copy of the object on the Windows Clipboard. You then can paste this copy on another slide. When you duplicate an object, PowerPoint makes a copy immediately and places it on the same slide. You then can drag the duplicate to the location you want.

Part 23: Copying, Pasting, and Duplicating Objects

1 Click the object you want to copy and click the **Copy** tool on the toolbar. You also can choose **Copy** from the **Edit** menu, or press **Ctrl+C**.

2 Display the slide in which you want to paste the copy, and click the **Paste** tool. You also can choose **Paste** from the **Edit** menu or press **Ctrl+C**. The copy of the object appears on the slide.

WHY WORRY?

The pasted object may be on top of other objects on this slide but this is normal. You can drag it to the position you want.

3 To duplicate an object, select it and then choose **Duplicate** from the **Edit** menu, or press **Ctrl+D**. The duplicated object is inserted on top of the original, but offset slightly so that you can tell the original from the duplicated copy. Drag the duplicated object to the position you want.

Resizing Objects

"Why would I do this?"

Sometimes you may want to resize an object to make more room on the slide, or to take up unused space. By dragging the resize handles, you can size any object the way you want.

Task 24: Resizing Objects

1 Select the object. You see the resize handles.

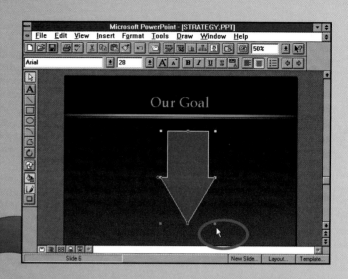

NOTE ▼

If you hold down the Ctrl key while dragging a resize handle, PowerPoint resizes the object from the center. If you hold down the Shift key while dragging, PowerPoint keeps the object's proportions while resizing. If you're resizing an AutoShape, note that some have a *control handle* (a diamond shape). Dragging the control handle adjusts the three-dimensional perspective.

2 Move the pointer to a resize handle. As you can see, the pointer changes shape to indicate what will happen when you drag the handle. If you position the pointer over the resize handle on the lower right, for example, PowerPoint indicates that you can size the object diagonally.

3 Try resizing an object. Click one of the resize handles, hold down the left mouse button, and drag.

WHY WORRY?

If you don't like the results of resizing an object, choose Undo from the Edit menu, or just click the Undo button.

Constraining an Object

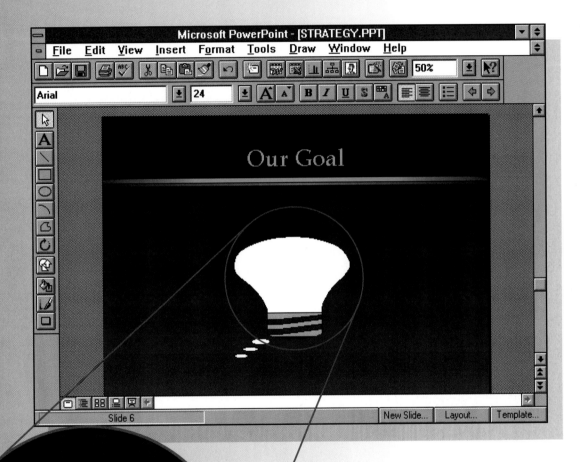

"Why would I do this?"

You've already moved objects—it's simple! You just click the object (or its border, if it's a text object or an object with no fill color), and drag. PowerPoint has some additional moving features you may find helpful, such as *constraining* the object to move horizontally or vertically while relocating. When you constrain an object, the diagonal resizing maintains the height to width relationship.

Task 25: Constraining an Object

1 Select the object you want to move.

2 To constrain the move horizontally or vertically while you move the object, press and hold down **Shift** and drag. If you drag horizontally, the width of the object changes but the height remains the same.

Moving with Grids and Guides

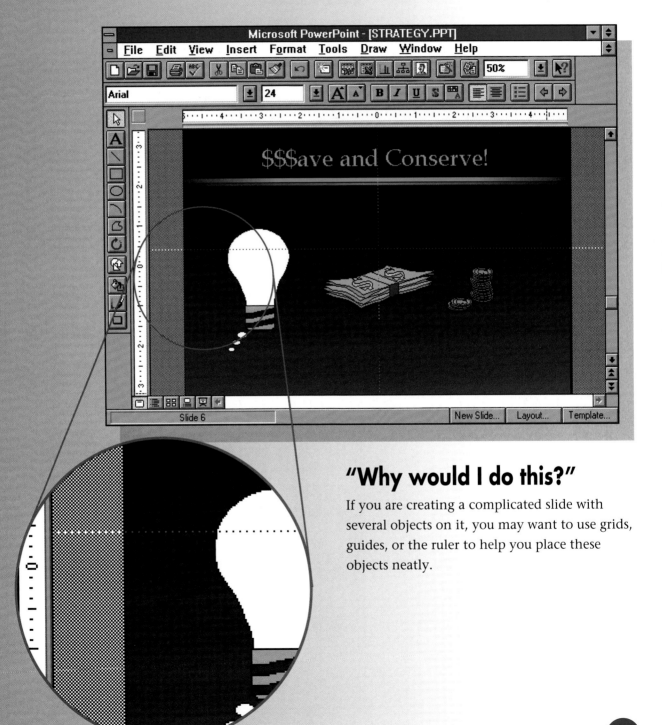

"Why would I do this?"

If you are creating a complicated slide with several objects on it, you may want to use grids, guides, or the ruler to help you place these objects neatly.

Task 26: Moving with Grids and Guides

1 The grid is an invisible checkboard of criss-crossed lines, 1/12th-inch apart. When you move an object close to a grid line, it snaps to the nearest grid line when you release the mouse button. To turn on the grid, choose **Snap to Grid** from the **Draw** menu. When the grid is turned on, you see a check mark on the menu next to the command. To turn off the guides, choose the command again.

2 The guides are like the grid, except there are only two—a horizontal guide and a vertical guide. By dragging a guide, you can position where you want, and after you do, the objects you insert will snap to the nearest guide. To insert the guides, choose **Guides** from the **View** menu. To turn off the guides, choose this command again.

3 The rulers give you a way to measure the pointer's location on-screen. When you turn on the rulers, a dotted line shows the pointer's current location. To turn on the rulers, choose **Ruler** from the **View** menu. To turn off the rulers, choose the same command again.

Stacking Objects

"Why would I do this?"

When you add objects to your slides, PowerPoint places the most recent object on top. But you may want to change the stack order, sending the top object back or bringing other objects forward. This affects how the objects look. In some cases, you may have to change the stack order to see through an object to the objects underneath. In this task, you learn how to experiment with the stack order by sending top objects backward and bringing other objects forward.

Task 27: Stacking Objects

1 On a slide that contains more than one object, select the top object.

2 Choose **Send Backward** from the **Draw** menu to send the object back one level. To send the object to the bottom of a stack of three or more objects, choose **Send to Back** from the **Draw** menu.

3 To bring an object forward one level, choose **Bring Forward** from the **Draw** menu. To bring an object to the top, choose **Bring to Front** from the **Draw** menu.

WHY WORRY?

If you're having trouble selecting an object beneath the stack, just press the Tab key until the object is selected.

Rotating Objects

"Why would I do this?"

You can create interesting visual effects by rotating objects. Use this effects to add meaning to your slide's message. You can rotate objects in two ways: free rotation or rotation by fixed amounts (90 degrees left or right).

Task 28: Rotating Objects

1 Select the object you want to rotate. If you want to rotate more than one object, you can group them.

NOTE ▼

If you want to rotate a clip art picture or other imported art, select the picture and choose Ungroup from the Draw menu. Then choose Regroup from the same menu to convert the picture into a PowerPoint object. If you can't ungroup and regroup the picture, you can't rotate it.

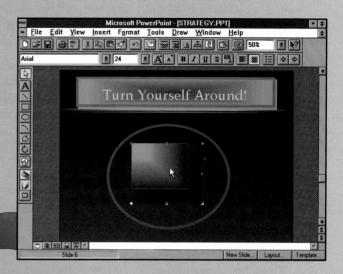

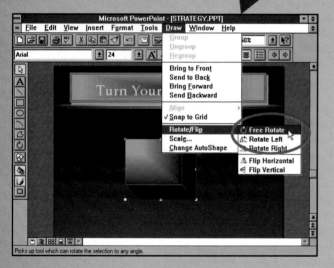

2 Choose **Rotate/Flip** from the **Draw** menu; a submenu appears. To rotate 90 degrees, choose **Rotate Left** or **Rotate Right**. If you choose **Free Rotate**, the pointer changes shape. Move it to one of the resize handles, and drag the handle in the direction you want to rotate the object.

NOTE ▼

If you want to free rotate an object, you can bypass the Draw menu by clicking the Free Rotate Tool on the Drawing toolbar.

Flipping
Objects

"Why would I do this?"

You can flip any PowerPoint object vertically or
horizontally. Use this effect to add a visual
comment on your slide's message.

Task 29: Flipping Objects

1 Select the object you want to flip.

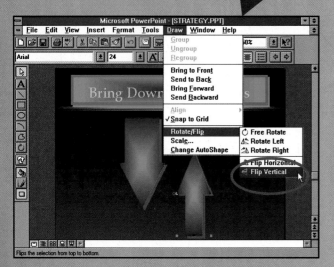

2 Choose **Rotate/Flip** from the **Draw** menu and then choose **Flip Horizontal** or **Flip Vertical** from the resulting submenu.

Working with Borders

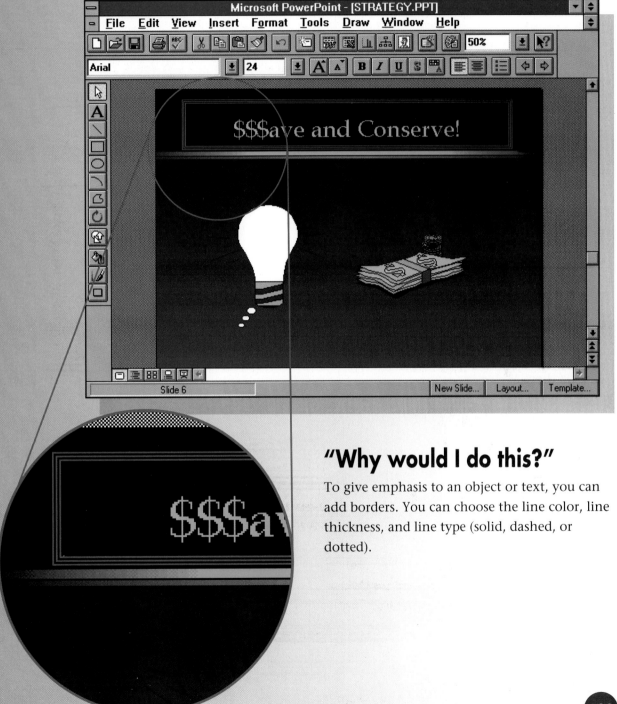

"Why would I do this?"

To give emphasis to an object or text, you can add borders. You can choose the line color, line thickness, and line type (solid, dashed, or dotted).

Task 30: Working with Borders

1 Select the object to which you want to add a border.

2 Choose **Colors and Lines** from the **Format** menu. You see the Colors and Lines dialog box. Click the down arrow next to the **Line** drop-down list box so that you can see the pop-up menu.

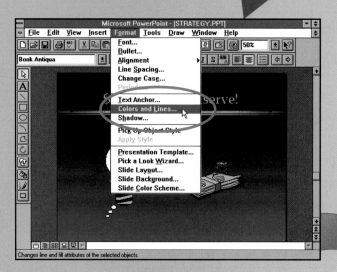

3 From the pop-up menu, click the line color you want. To see additional colors, click **Other Color** to see additional colors; click one of them and choose **OK**. The Line text box now shows the color you've chosen.

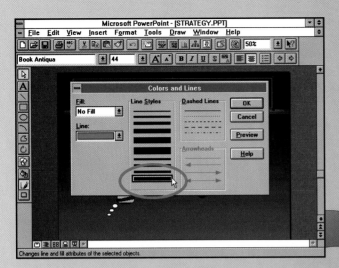

4 In the **Line Styles** area, click a line thickness or line style. You also can choose a dashed or dotted line in the **Dashed Lines** area.

5 Click **OK** to confirm your choice. The object now has a border!

Working with Fills and Patterns

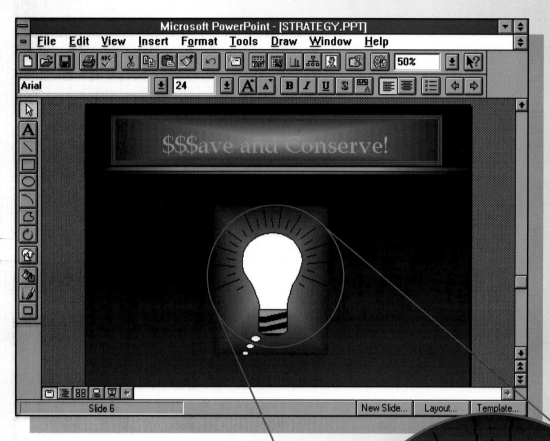

"Why would I do this?"

You can add additional emphasis to an object by using a fill color or pattern that differs from the slide background. You can choose from beautiful shaded fills, patterns of all kinds, or dozens of colors.

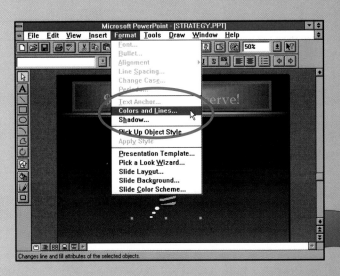

1 Select the object to which you want to add a fill color or pattern and choose **Colors and Lines** from the **Format** menu. You see the Colors and Lines dialog box. Click the down arrow next to the **Fill** drop-down list box so that you can see the palette.

2 From palette, click the color you want and click **OK**. You also can click **Shaded**, **Pattern**, or **Other Color** for the background. If you choose **Pattern** or **Color**, click the pattern or fill color you want and click **OK**. If you choose **Shaded**, the Shaded Fill dialog box appears.

> **NOTE** ▼
>
> You can choose more than one fill effect. Try choosing a Shaded effect and a color.

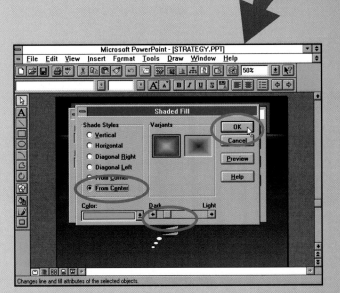

3 You see this dialog box only if you chose the Shaded option. Click one of the Shaded Styles options, and click one of the Variants options. If you want, you can choose a color from the Color drop-down list box, and drag the scroll box to adjust the darkness of the shaded effect. When you finish choosing your shaded effect, click **OK**. The Fill box shows the fill effect you've chosen. Click **OK** to return to your slide and see the result.

TASK 32
Adding Shadows

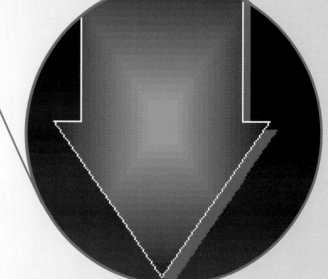

"Why would I do this?"

Shadow effects provide another way to give emphasis to objects. Used sparingly, they can call attention to the aspects of your presentation you want to feature. With a shadow, an object appears to float on the surface of the slide.

1 Select the object to which you want to apply a shadow. This task uses an AutoShape arrow for an example. Click the **Shadow On/Off** tool on the Drawing toolbar.

WHY WORRY?

If you don't like the shadow effect and want to remove it, just click the Shadow On/Off tool again.

2 To change the shadow color, choose **Shadow** from the **Format** menu.

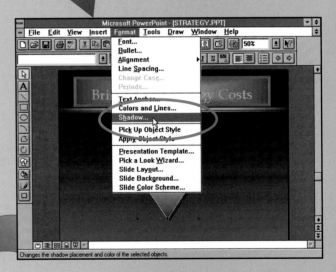

3 Choose the color you want from the **Color** box, and click **OK**.

TASK 33

Adding an Embossed Effect

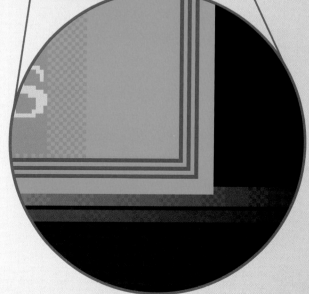

"Why would I do this?"

A variation on PowerPoint's shadow effect, *embossing* uses extra shadow to produce a special effect. Use embossing on objects that have the same color as the slide background for the best results.

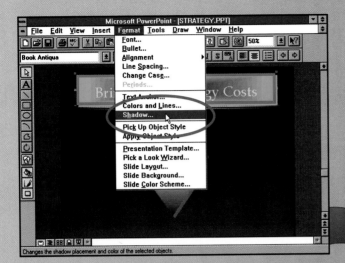

1 Select the object that you want to emboss and choose **Shadow** from the **Format** menu. You see the Shadow dialog box.

2 Click the down arrow next to the Color text box, and choose **Embossed** from the drop-down list, and then click **OK**.

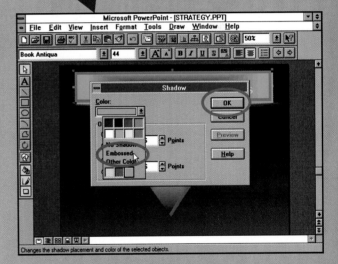

TASK 34
Using Format Painter

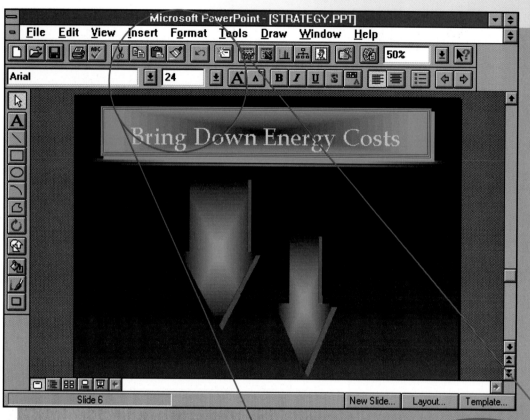

"Why would I do this?"

Suppose that you have added attributes such as borders, a fill color, and a pattern to an object. You like the results, and you want to use them elsewhere. To avoid having to go through steps again, use *Format Painter*. Format Painter copies the attributes from one object to another.

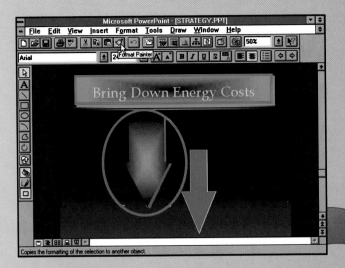

1 Select the object whose attributes you want to copy. Try selecting one of the objects that you enhanced in the previous Tasks. Click the **Format Painter** tool on the toolbar. The pointer becomes a paint brush.

2 Click the object to which you want to apply the copied attributes. The object now reflects the colors you copied using the Format Painter tool.

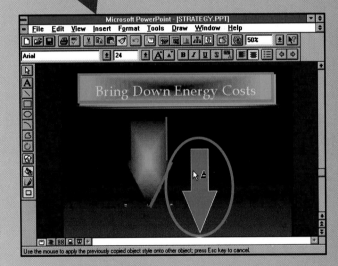

PART IV

Working with Text

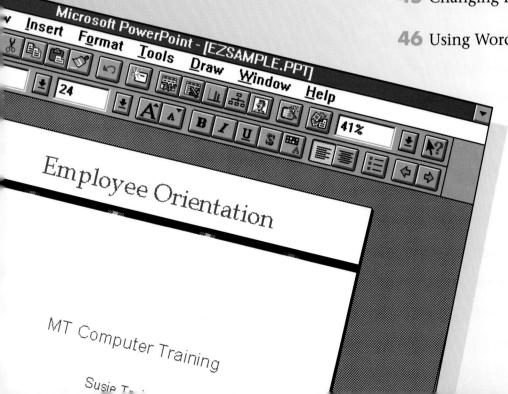

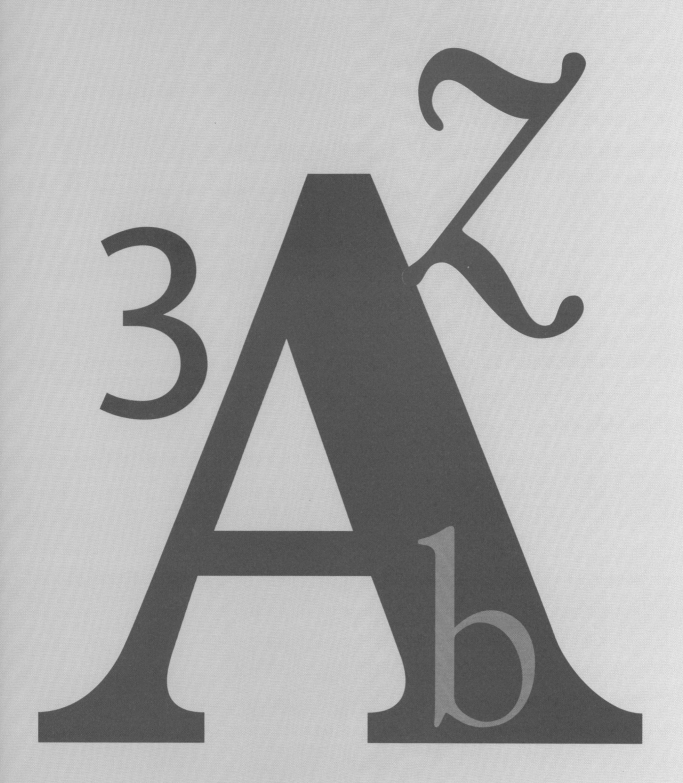

Text should be used sparingly in a presentation—it's not necessary to explain everything on a slide. That's what your spoken remarks are for! The text on the slides should be concise, legible, helpful, and—above all—visually appealing.

You can add text anywhere in a PowerPoint presentation—not just in the text placeholders inserted by AutoLayout. You even can add text within an AutoShape so that the shape expands to accommodate the text.

PowerPoint takes care of much of the visual appeal automatically. When you attach a template to a PowerPoint presentation, the template specifies the font (design) of the text, as well as its size (in printer's points), its color, and its alignment (flush left or centered). These defaults are fine for most purposes. You may, however, want to change them for emphasis.

TASK 35
Adding Text Anywhere

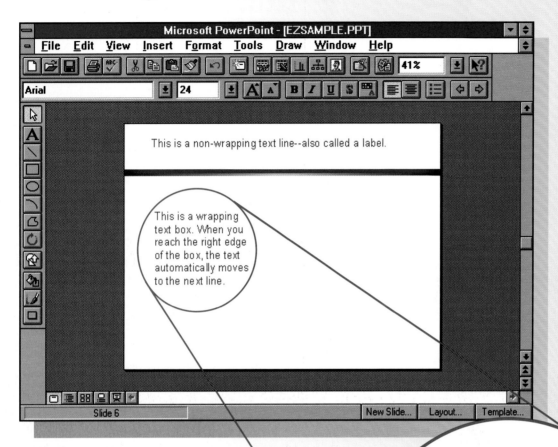

"Why would I do this?"

Sometimes you may want to add explanatory text to a slide. For example, you may want to add a caption to a picture. You can add text anywhere using the Text tool on the Drawing toolbar. You can add text in two ways: with or without word wrapping. *Word wrapping* automatically "wraps" the text to the next line if the text won't fit on a single line within the box you've drawn.

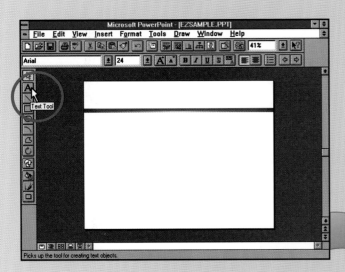

1 Click the **Text** tool on the toolbar.

2 Move the pointer to where you want the text to appear, click the left mouse button to activate the insertion point, and begin typing. Because word wrapping is not on, PowerPoint enlarges the box on the right to make room for your text.

NOTE ▼

You can add word wrapping to text entered without it. Choose Text Anchor from the Format menu. Click Word-Wrap Text in Object, and click OK.

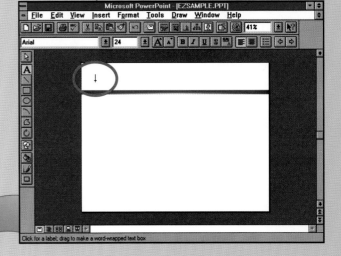

3 Now try entering some text with word wrapping. Move the pointer to where you want the text to appear, and click and drag to the right and down. This makes a box. Release the mouse button. When you drag a box, the text wraps within the box's right edge. Click within the box and type the text you want. As you can see, PowerPoint wraps the text within the box. PowerPoint enlarges the box on the bottom to make room, if necessary.

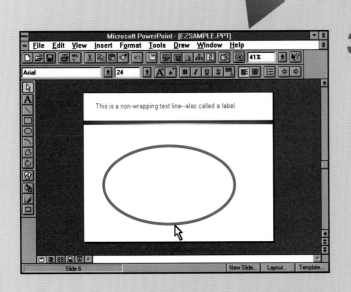

TASK 36

Adding Text to an AutoShape

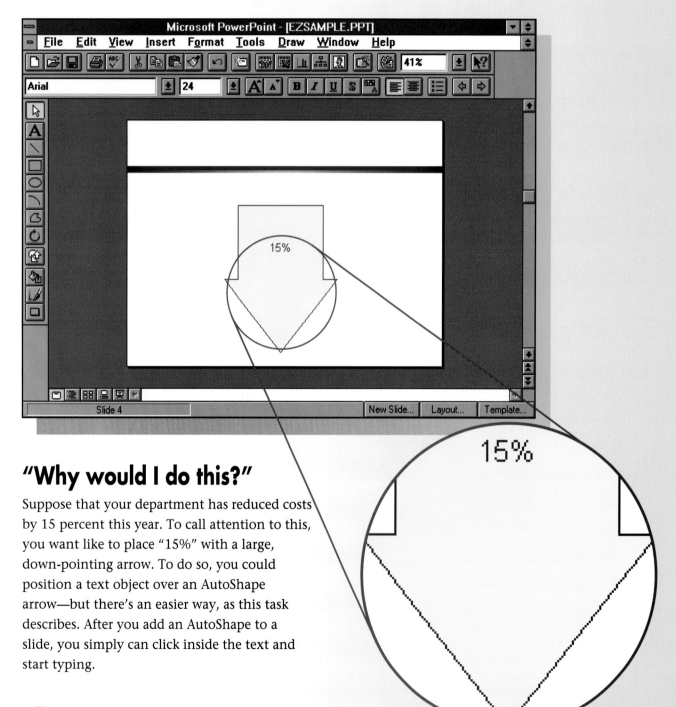

"Why would I do this?"

Suppose that your department has reduced costs by 15 percent this year. To call attention to this, you want like to place "15%" with a large, down-pointing arrow. To do so, you could position a text object over an AutoShape arrow—but there's an easier way, as this task describes. After you add an AutoShape to a slide, you simply can click inside the text and start typing.

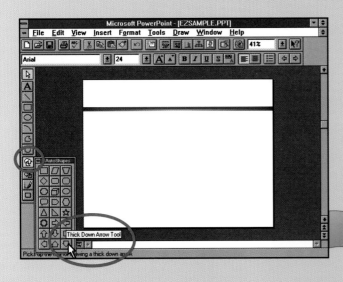

1 Click the **AutoShape** tool on the Drawing toolbar. In the palette that appears, click the shape you want to add. For this task, you can add a thick down arrow.

2 To insert the shape on-screen, click and drag the mouse to proportion the arrow to the size you want.

WHY WORRY?

If the text you type does not fit within the shape, choose Text Anchor from the Format menu. Then do one of the following: If the text looks good now, click the Adjust Object Size to Fit Text option. If you want the text to change to fit the object, click Word-wrap Text in Object. Click OK to confirm your choice.

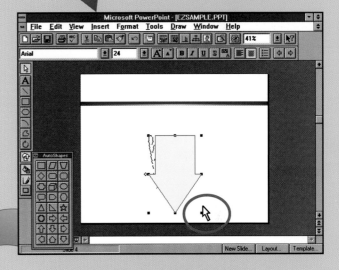

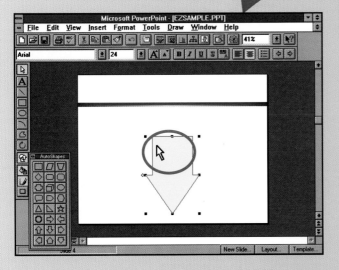

3 Click the pointer in the shape and begin typing. For this example, type **15%**. PowerPoint adds the text to the shape.

TASK 37
Anchoring the Text

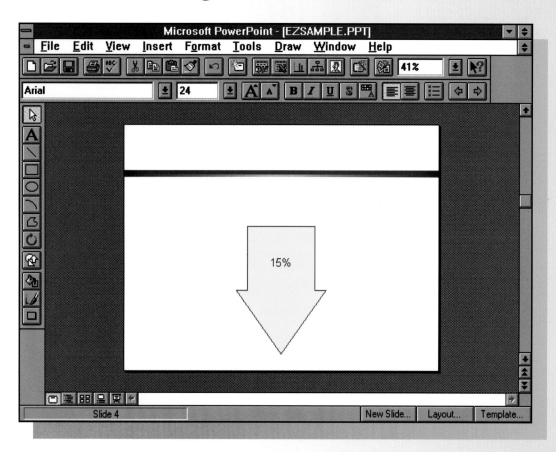

"Why would I do this?"

When you add text to a shape, PowerPoint applies automatically its defaults for *anchoring* the text. You can think of anchoring as if the program were pinning down the text in a certain part of the shape. You can anchor the text at the top, middle, or bottom of the shape, and you also can choose centering options. Additionally, you can turn on word wrapping. This is needed if the text you've typed is too long to fit within the shape.

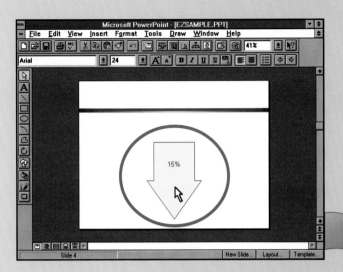

1 Select the object that contains text you want to anchor.

2 Choose **Text Anchor** from the **Format** menu. You see the Anchor Text dialog box.

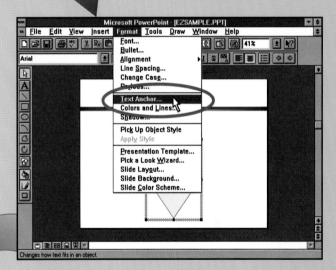

3 In the **Anchor Point** drop-down list box, choose the anchoring point you want. You can anchor the text in the Top, Middle, or Bottom of the shape. If you choose one of the Centered options (Top Centered, Middle Centered, or Bottom Centered), PowerPoint will center the text between the right and left edges of the shape.

Task 37: Anchoring the Text

4 In the **Box Margins** area, adjust the space between the text and the shape edges, if you want (but these default settings are fine for most purposes).

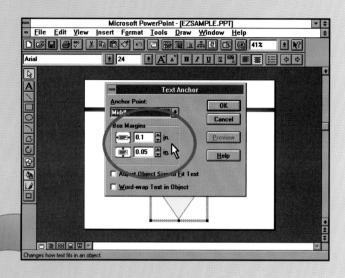

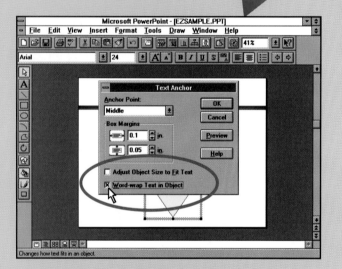

5 If you want to wrap the text within the shape, click the **Word-wrap Text in Object** check box. This is a good choice if the text you typed is too long and moves outside the shape's edge. Alternatively, click **Adjust Object Size to Fit Text** to make the object fit to the text. This is a good option if the text looks good now and you want the shape to adjust to the text. Click **OK** to see the effects of anchoring the text.

Deleting Text and Undoing the Deletion

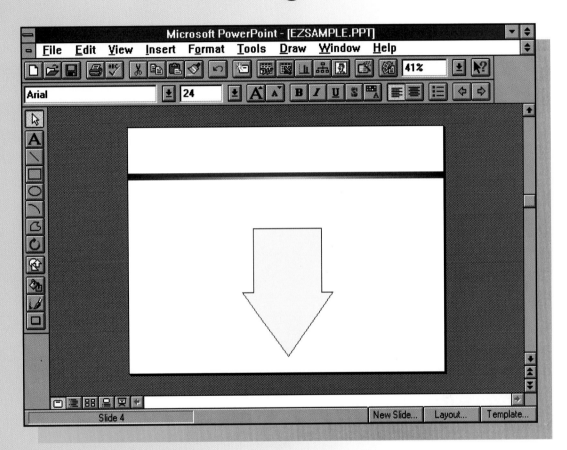

"Why would I do this?"

Sometimes you type text and later decide to delete it. If you're typing the text, you can delete what you typed just by pressing the Backspace key; however, PowerPoint supplies other ways to delete text too. You also can undelete text if you deleted something accidentally. This task shows you how to delete text using the Clear and Undo commands.

Task 38: Deleting Text and Undoing the Deletion

1 Select the text you want to delete.

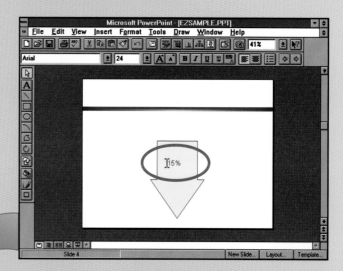

2 To delete the text, you can press **Delete** on the keyboard, or choose **Clear** from the **Edit** menu.

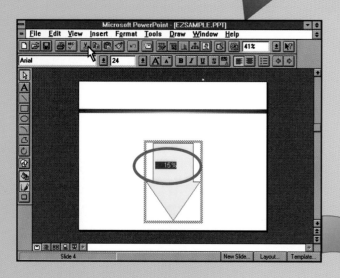

3 To undo text you accidentally deleted, click the **Undo** tool on the toolbar.

> **NOTE** ▼
>
> You can only undo the last action you performed. You cannot delete text, move some text, and then go back and undo the deletion.

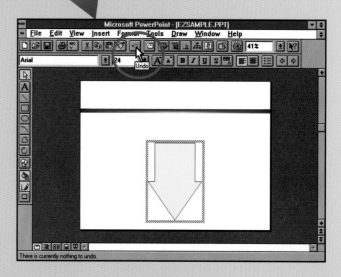

TASK 39
Copying and Pasting Text

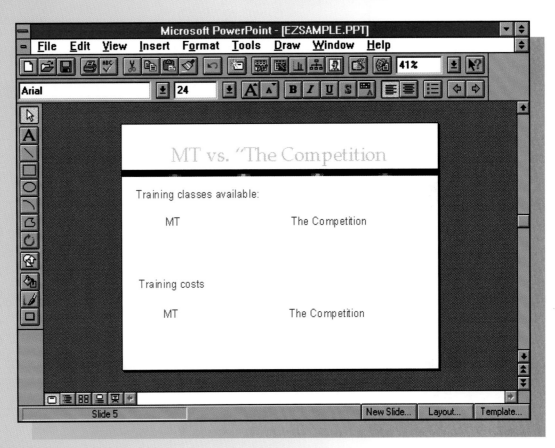

"Why would I do this?"

If you want to repeat text in another place in PowerPoint, you don't need to type it twice. You can copy it to the new location using the Copy and Paste commands on the Edit menu. You also can copy text using the mouse; however, where the Copy and Paste commands enable you to copy text from one slide and paste it into another slide, the mouse technique, called *drag-and-drop*, only enables you to copy and move text within the same slide.

Task 39: Copying and Pasting Text

1 On the slide that contains text you want to copy, select the text you want to copy and then click the **Copy** tool on the toolbar. Alternatively, you can choose **Copy** from the **Edit** menu or press **Ctrl+C**. PowerPoint copies the text you selected to the Clipboard. The Clipboard is a temporary storage area for text and objects you copy or cut from a slide.

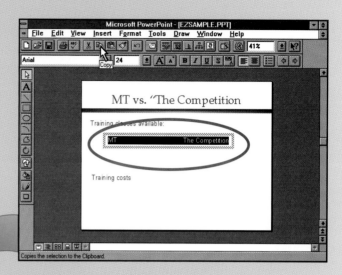

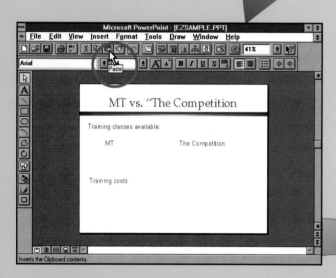

2 To place a copy of the text, click the insertion point in the place you want the text to appear, and then click the **Paste** tool on the toolbar or choose **Paste** from the **Edit** menu (You also can press **Ctrl+V**.) A copy of the text appears. You can move and size the text as necessary.

> **NOTE** ▼
>
> With the Clipboard technique you just learned, you can copy text to another slide—or even to another presentation or another application.

3 To use the drag-and-drop method, select the text you want to copy, and then press and hold down **Ctrl.** The mouse pointer changes shape to show that the pointer is "carrying" the text. When you have moved the pointer to the end of the same object, release the mouse button. The text is copied. (This works only for one text object in one slide.)

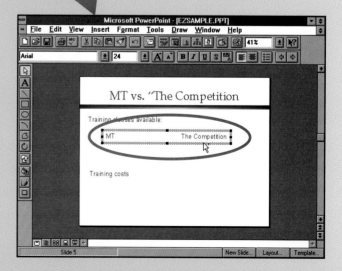

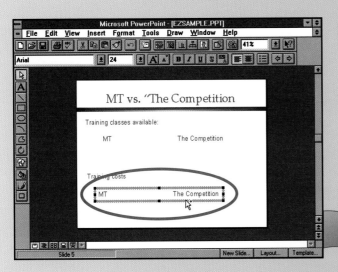

4 Click and drag the text to the desired location. Use the outline of the text area as a guide for placing the copied text.

5 Release the mouse button. A copy of the selected text appears at the location indicated by the pointer.

WHY WORRY?

If you moved the text rather than copied it when using the mouse, remember to hold down the Ctrl key while dragging. Click Undo and try again.

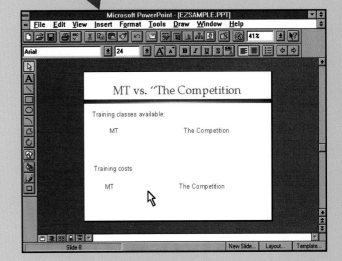

Moving Text

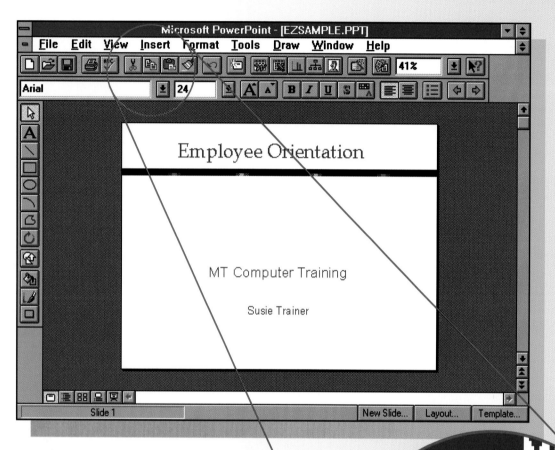

"Why would I do this?"

If you want to move text from one place to
another, you don't need to delete it and then
retype it. You can move the text using the Cut
and Paste commands (by placing it on the
Clipboard) or you can move it using the drag-
and-drop mouse technique.

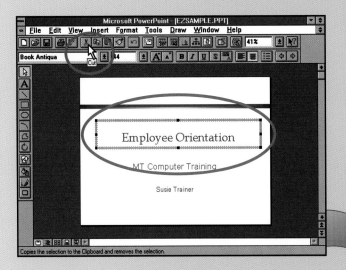

1 Select the text you want to move and then click the **Cut** tool on the toolbar or choose **Cut** from the **Edit** menu. You also can press **Ctrl+X**.

NOTE ▼

With the Clipboard technique you just learned, you can copy text to another slide—or even to another presentation or another application. When moving text on the same slide, you can use the drag-and-drop method explained in the next step.

2 Click the place in which you want to move the text and then click the **Paste** tool on the toolbar. Alternatively, you can choose **Paste** from the **Edit** menu or press **Ctrl+V**.

NOTE ▼

The mouse moving technique works only within a single text object. You can't use this technique to move text to another slide or presentation.

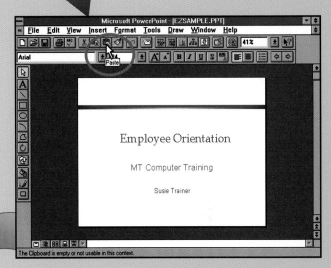

3 If you want, you can use the mouse technique rather than the Clipboard technique. To do this, select the text you want to move, and drag to the place you want it to appear. As you can see, the mouse pointer changes shape to show that the pointer is "carrying" the text. When the pointer is in the place you want the text to appear, release the mouse button.

TASK 41
Finding and Replacing Text

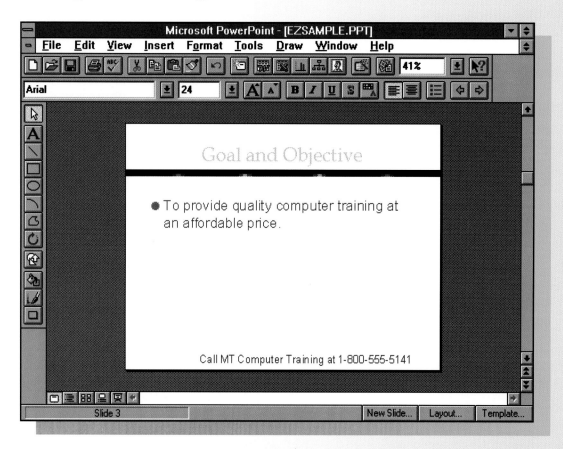

"Why would I do this?"

Suppose that you have just finished a presentation that includes your company telephone number—and then your boss comes in and says, "Oh, by the way, we changed our 800 number yesterday! It's now 1-800-555-5142." With PowerPoint's Find command, you can quickly locate text anywhere in your presentation. With the Replace command, you can ask PowerPoint to go through your presentation and substitute the text for the old text.

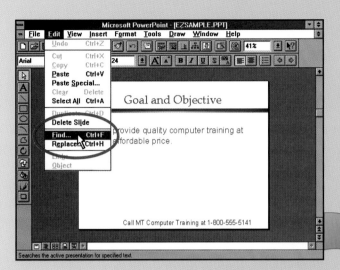

1 To search locate specific text in your presentation, choose **Find** from the **Edit** menu. The Find dialog box appears.

2 In the **Find What** text box, type the text you want to find. If you want PowerPoint to find the word only if it contains the capitalization you typed (for example, "Brown" but not "brown"), click the **Match Case** check box. If you want PowerPoint to skip the text you've typed unless it stands alone as a whole word (for example, "ever" but not "every"), click the **Whole Word** option.

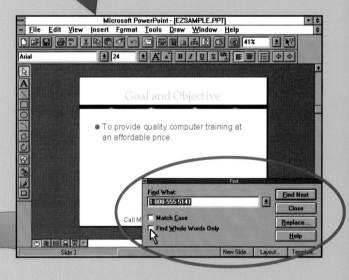

3 Click **Find Next** to begin the search. If PowerPoint finds a match, the program displays the slide and highlights the word. You then can click **Close** to close the Find dialog box, or **Find Next** to look for the next occurrence of the word.

NOTE ▼

If you didn't start the search at the beginning of your presentation, you may see a dialog box asking if you want to continue from the beginning. Click Yes to make sure that PowerPoint searches the entire presentation.

133

4 To search and replace text, choose Replace from the Edit menu. The Replace dialog box appears.

NOTE ▼

You also can click Replace in the Find dialog box to display the Replace options. If you used the Find dialog box previously, you see the text you searched for in the Find What box.

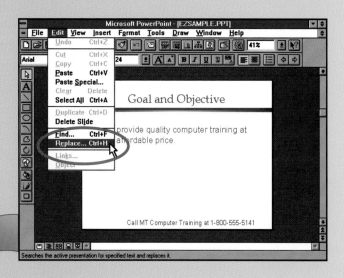

5 In the **Find What** text box, type the text you want to find. In the **Replace With** text box, type the text you want to replace it with. Click **Find Next** to begin the procedure.

NOTE ▼

You can specify that PowerPoint matches the case or the whole word, just as in using the Find command.

6 When PowerPoint finds the first instance of the text, the program highlights the text on the slide. Click **Replace** to replace this instance, **Find Next** to skip this instance and go on to the next one, or **Replace All** to make all the replacements without confirmation. When PowerPoint has completed the Find and Replace procedure, click **Close** to close the dialog box.

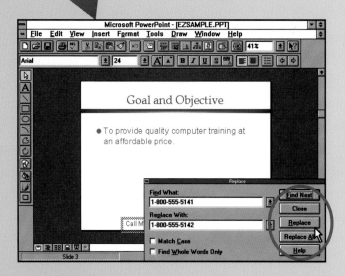

Formatting Text

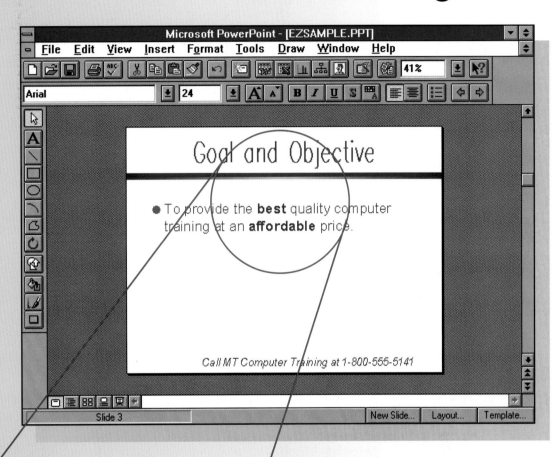

"Why would I do this?"

PowerPoint automatically formats your text in line with the design philosophy of the template you're using. This includes fonts, font sizes, and emphases, such as italic and bold. Sometimes, however, you may want to override the template's default formats. If you want to emphasize one item in a bulleted list, for example, you might want to apply boldface formatting to this item to make it stand out. This task teaches the basics of formatting your text with fonts, font sizes, emphases, and cool effects, such as shadows and embossing.

135

Task 42: Formatting Text

1 Select the text you want to format.

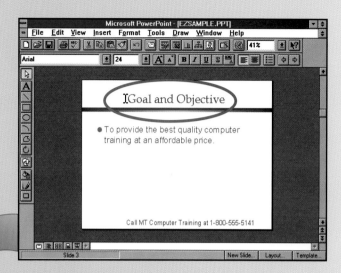

2 To make the text larger, click the **Increase Font Size** tool on the toolbar to increase the font size. To make the text smaller, click the **Decrease Font Size** tool on the toolbar. Use these tools until the text is the size you want.

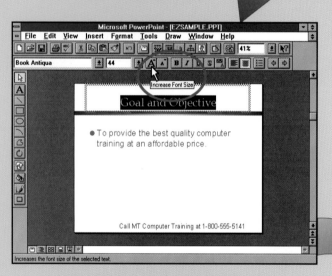

3 To make the text bold, select the text, and click the **Bold** tool on the toolbar. To unbold the text, just click the **Bold** tool again.

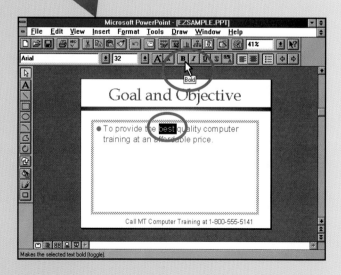

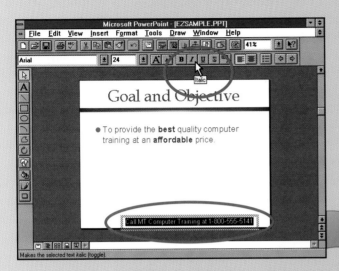

4 To make the text italic, select the text, and click the **Italic** tool on the toolbar. Click it again to turn off italic.

5 To underline the text, select the text, and click the **Underline** tool on the toolbar. Click it again to turn off underlining.

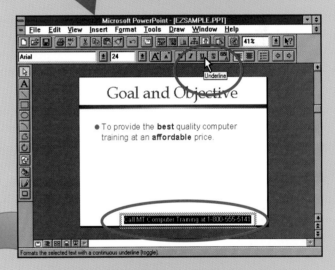

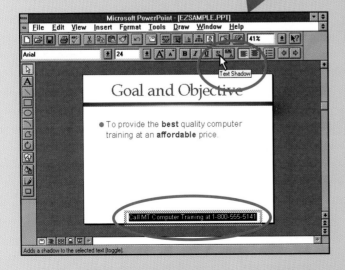

6 To give the text a shadow effect, select the text, and click the **Text Shadow** tool on the toolbar to turn on shadowing. Click it again to turn off shadowing.

7 To change the color of the text, select the text, and click the **Text Color** tool on the toolbar. A small palette of text colors appears. Click the color you want.

> **NOTE** ▼
>
> If you want to see more colors, click Other Color. When the Other Color dialog box appears, click the color you want, and then click OK.

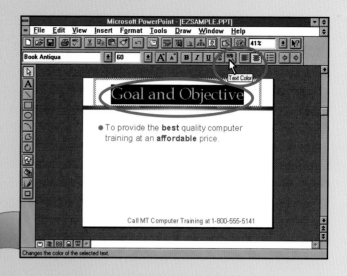

8 To change the font, select the text, and then click the down arrow beside the font name box to display a list of available fonts. Click the font you want to use.

9 There are a few formats you can't choose with the tools on the toolbar (embossing and superscript or subscript). To choose these formats, select the text to enhance and choose **Font** from the **Format** menu. You see the Font dialog box. Choose from Emboss, Superscript, or Subscript. PowerPoint enters an offset percentage. To change this, click the **Offset** arrows. Click **OK** to close the Font dialog box.

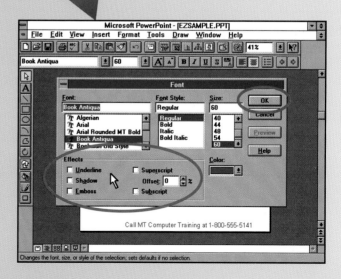

TASK 43

Working with Bullets

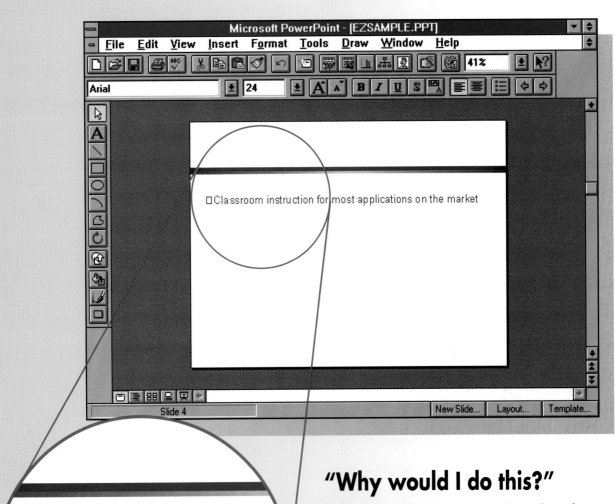

"Why would I do this?"

Bullets are useful when presenting a list of items. PowerPoint enters them automatically when you use a bulleted list placeholder. However, you can place bullets in front of any text you type, including text in the text objects you create using the Text tool. You also can choose any character you want as a bullet.

Task 43: Working with Bullets

1 On a blank slide, click the **Text** tool on the toolbar and type a line of text on the slide.

> **NOTE** ▼
>
> If you want to change all the bullets in a bulleted list object, select the object before choosing Bullet from the Format menu. The choices you make apply to all the bullets in the list.

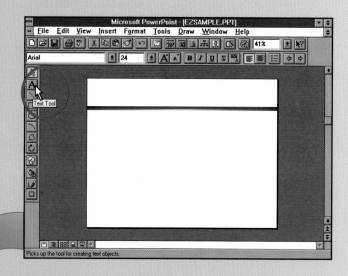

2 Select the text with the bullet, and then click the **Bullet** tool on the toolbar. PowerPoint adds a bullet to your text.

> **WHY WORRY?**
>
> If you don't like the bullet, just click the Bullet tool again. The bullet disappears.

3 To change the bullet, choose **Bullet** from the **Format** menu. The Bullet dialog box appears. The current bullet is highlighted. To change the font, choose a font name in the **Bullets From** drop-down list box. To choose another color for the bullet, click the **Special Color** check box and choose a bullet color from the list box. You also can increase or decrease the size of the bullet by clicking the arrows in the **Size** drop-down list box. To confirm your bullet choices, click **OK**.

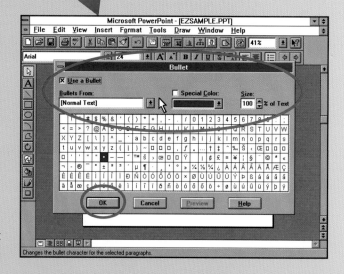

Changing Text Alignment

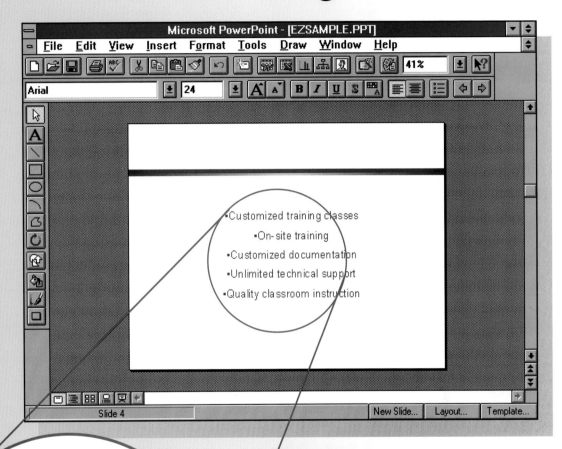

"Why would I do this?"

PowerPoint's templates include default alignment settings for placeholders such as titles (titles usually are centered). These settings are fine for most purposes; however, you might want to choose a different alignment if you create a new text object with the Text tool. You can choose flush left, centered, flush right, or justified (both margins even).

141

Task 44: Changing Text Alignment

1 Select the text you want to align differently. (By default, this text is aligned flush left.) Click the **Centered Alignment** tool on the toolbar.

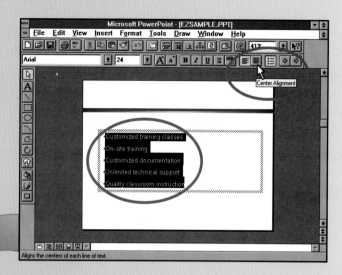

2 To choose justified and flush right alignment, you must use the Alignment command. Choose **Alignment** from the **Format** menu. A cascade menu with a dot indicating the current alignment appears. From the submenu, click the alignment you want.

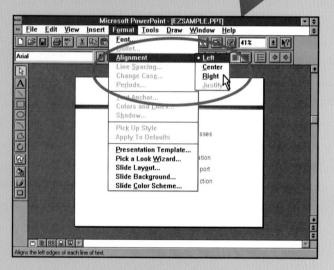

> **NOTE** ▼
>
> Avoid justified alignment (both margins even). With the short line lengths on your slides, PowerPoint may leave large areas blank between words in order to even out the lines, and this doesn't always look good.

Changing Line Spacing

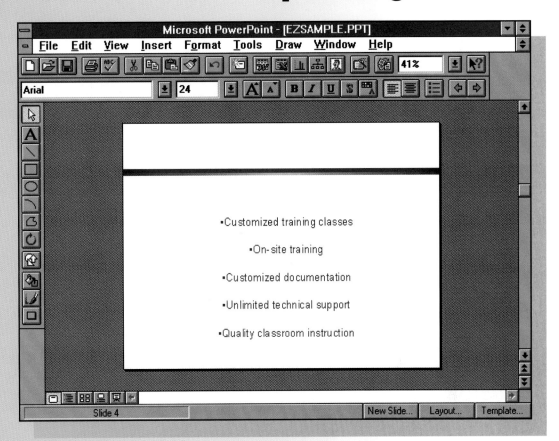

"Why would I do this?"

When typing a list, you might want to increase the line space between each item. Rather than pressing Enter to leave a blank line, you can adjust the line spacing. You also can tell PowerPoint to enter a certain amount of blank space automatically when you press Enter after typing a line.

Task 45: Changing Line Spacing

1 Select the line of text before or after which you want to change the line spacing.

NOTE ▼

If you're changing the spacing in a bulleted list, select the bulleted list object so that your choices will affect the whole list.

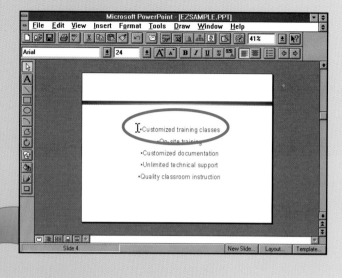

2 Choose **Line Spacing** from the **Format** menu. You see the Line Spacing dialog box.

NOTE ▼

If you want, you can specify spacing options in printer's points (72 pointers per inch) rather than lines. In the Lines drop-down list box, choose Points.

3 To change the line spacing, click the up or down arrows to change the number in the **Line Spacing** spin box. If you want, you can add space before or after the lines in the **Before Paragraph** or **After Paragraph** boxes. Click **OK** to confirm your choice.

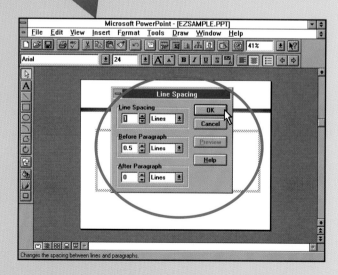

TASK 46
Using WordArt

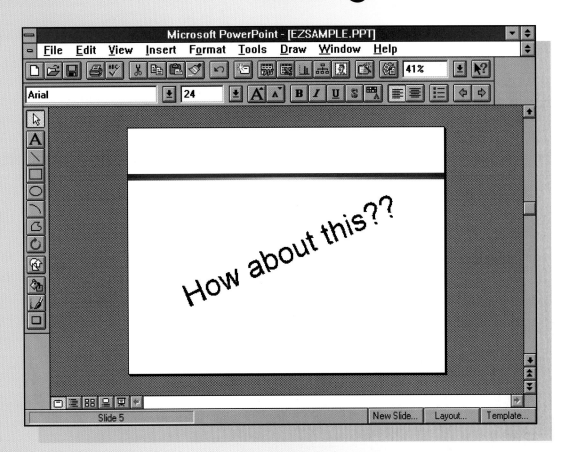

"Why would I do this?"

To call attention to important messages in your document, you may want to add special text effects, such as slanting or curving the text. Microsoft WordArt is an application included with PowerPoint that enables you to choose from a variety of special effects. It works best with one or two words or a short phrase.

Task 46: Using WordArt

1 Display a slide that contains a large blank area. Choose **Object** from the **Insert** menu. You see the Insert Object dialog box.

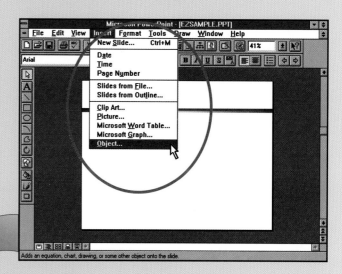

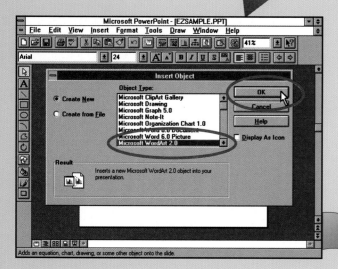

2 In the **Object Type** list, click **Microsoft WordArt 2.0**, and then click **OK**. PowerPoint inserts a Microsoft WordArt object on your slide, and you see the Enter Your Text Here dialog box that enables you to type text. The text Your Text Here shows what your text will look like with the current settings.

NOTE ▼

When you start WordArt, this application replaces PowerPoint's menu and toolbars.

3 Type some text. Keep it short! To see what the text looks like, click the **Update Display** button. The text you typed appears on-screen.

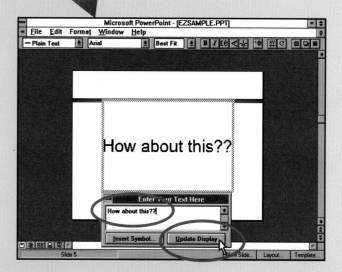

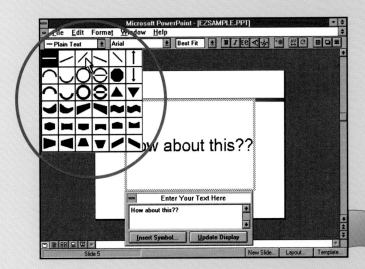

4 Now try choosing a special effect. Click the down arrow next to the Style selection box. You see a menu of special effects. Click the **Slant Up** option. The effect you chose in step 4 shows on-screen. You also can change the font by choosing a new font from the Font selection box that is next to the Style selection box.

5 To exit WordArt, just click the slide background. You see your WordArt effect on the slide.

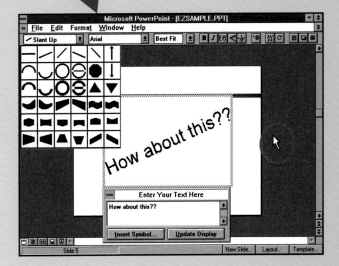

PART V

Working with Graphs and Visuals

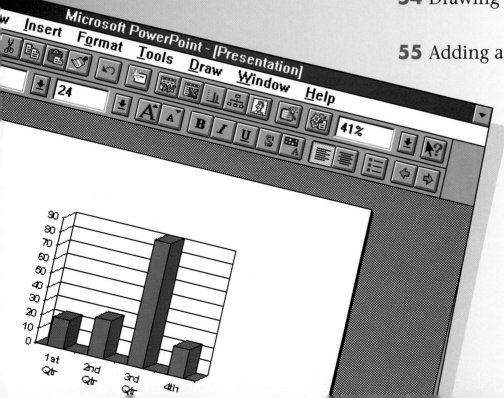

PowerPoint comes with *Microsoft Graph*, a business graph program that has many capabilities. For a presentation, however, you should keep your graphs simple. Your goal: Highlight the trends you want your audience to see.

If you're new to graphs, you might feel overwhelmed by all the Microsoft Graph options. But making a great-looking graph is easy. You just type your data in place of the sample data that Graph provides. Thanks to Graph's AutoFormats, you don't have to worry about choosing formatting options. Graph does the work for you! One important decision, however, is left up to you: choosing the correct graph type for your data. You can choose from the following:

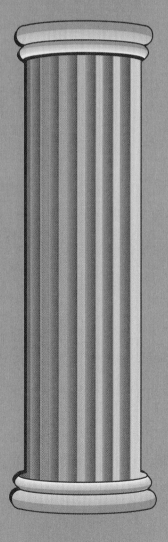

- *Area Graphs* show your data with a filled-in shape. Choose an area graph when you want to convey the magnitude of the data you're describing. This is particularly effective when you are showing two or three data series. Each data series adds mass to the area. You can use this to show how three products have added up to increasing sales, year after year.

- *Bar Graphs* show your data in bars, horizontally across the screen. Choose a bar graph when you want to list items and show their quantities. You can use this to show the number of employees in each department of a firm.

- *Column Graphs* look like bar graphs, except the bars are vertical. Use a column graph when you want to show how items change over time. You can use a column graph to show how customer complaints have decreased for each of the last twelve months.

- *Line Graphs* trace fluctuations over time. Choose a line graph to show changes in prices, rates, or other numbers. You can use this to show how your sales have fared, compared to your competitors, over the past five years.

- *Pie Graphs* show the parts of a whole. You can "explode" a slide for emphasis by drawing it apart from the rest of the pie. A pie graph can only show one data series. You can use a pie graph to show how your firm spent its profits last year (for example, 23 percent for research and development, 48 percent for dividends, and so on).

- *Doughnut Graphs* resemble pie graphs, but they can show more than one data series. (These graphs are widely used in Asia.) You can use this to show how proportions of a whole have changed; for example, your firm invested 23 percent of its profits in R & D last year, but 34 percent this year.

- *Scatter, Surface, and Radar Graphs* have special purposes in scientific and technical fields. Use these graph types to illustrate correlation and comparison, such as illustrating how the weather affects retail business.

Graphs aren't the only way to spice up a slide! You can use clip art and draw shapes. Microsoft Clip Art provides a wide variety of clip art from which to choose.

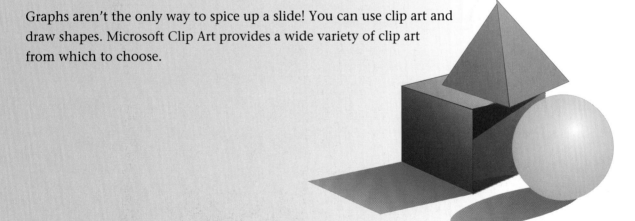

Adding a Graph Anywhere

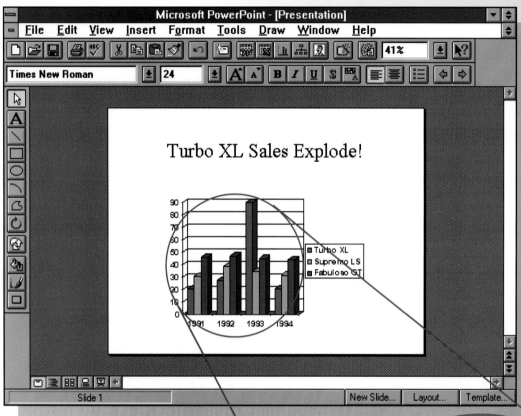

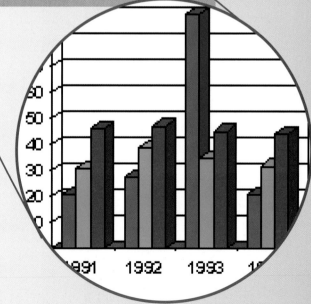

"Why would I do this?"

You easily can add a graph to any slide, even one that does not have a graph placeholder. The Insert Graph tool enables you to define and insert a graph on any slide in your presentation. Once you insert the graph, you can fill out the datasheet to reflect your information.

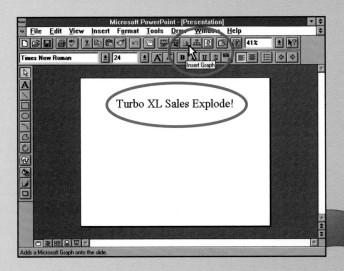

1 Create a new slide with the Title Only AutoLayout. Click the title text area and type the title **Turbo XL Sales Explode!** Now click the **Insert Graph** tool. PowerPoint starts Microsoft Graph. You see the sample chart and datasheet window.

NOTE ▼

To make more room for the row headings, click the line dividing the first column and column A; An arrow pointing both ways indicates that you can now widen the column. Drag right to make room for the headings.

2 To create your graph, you just modify the sample data. To do this, click the cell in row 1 containing the heading **East**. Type the new heading. It automatically replaces the existing heading. Press the **down arrow** to edit the next heading. Do the same for the third heading. To enter the column headings, click the cell in column A containing the heading **1st Qtr**. Type the new heading, and then press **Tab** to edit the next heading. Just use the sample numbers for the data.

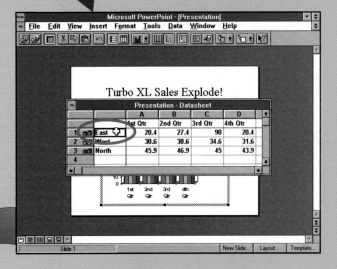

3 Click the **Datasheet** tool on the toolbar to hide the datasheet. This enables you to see your graph. If you need to redisplay the datasheet, click the **Datasheet** tool again.

WHY WORRY?

If you accidentally click on the screen but not on the graph and the Graph toolbar disappears, just double-click the graph again to display the Graph toolbar.

TASK 48

Choosing a Graph Type with AutoFormat

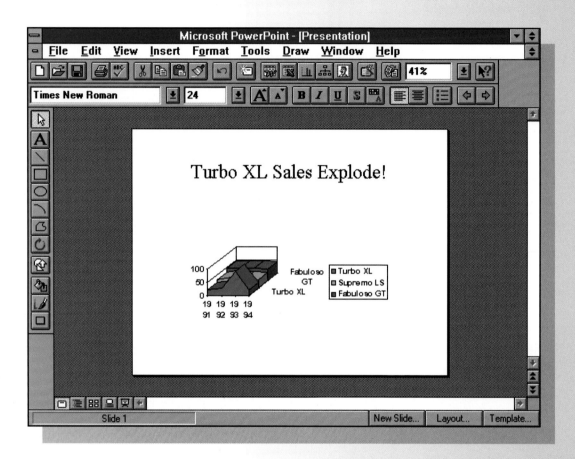

"Why would I do this?"

If Graph's default graph type (a three-dimensional column chart) isn't the right choice for your data, you can change the graph type without retyping your data. When you choose a new graph type with AutoFormat, you also get just the right formats for your graph—including grid lines, legend location, fonts, and other options. Let Graph do the work for you!

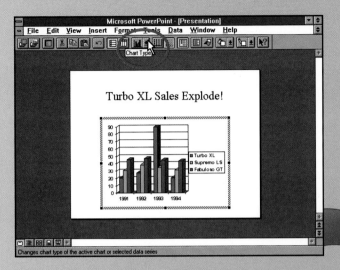

1 If necessary, double-click your graph to activate Microsoft Graph. Click the **Chart Type** tool. You see a pop-up menu with graph types.

NOTE ▼

On the left, you see two-dimensional graph types. On the right, you see their three-dimensional counterparts.

2 Click one of the graph types to change your graph. AutoFormat selects the appropriate formats automatically. Try clicking the **Area Chart** AutoFormat.

WHY WORRY?

If you don't like the change that AutoFormat has made, just click the Undo tool to restore the previous graph type.

WHY WORRY?

The Chart Type tool lists the most commonly used graph formats. You can choose from many more by choosing AutoFormat from the Format menu.

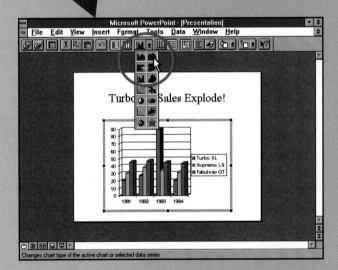

TASK 49

Displaying the Data by Rows or Columns

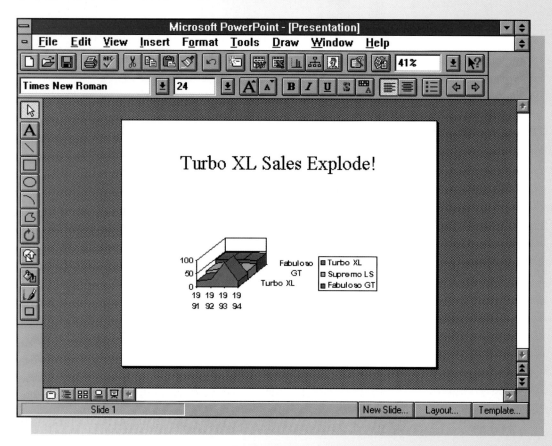

"Why would I do this?"

When you type your data in the Graph datasheet, you type your data series in rows. Graph, however, can display your data as if you typed the data series in columns. Sometimes, this produces an effect that can help you highlight the trend you want to emphasize.

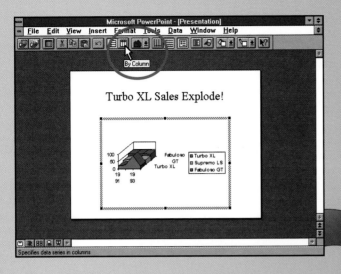

1 Display the graph you created in Task 48, and then double-click on the graph to switch to Graph. With your graph displayed in Graph, click the **By Column** tool on the toolbar. Graph now displays your data as if you had typed the data series in columns rather than rows. This highlights the increase in the Turbo XL's sales.

2 Click the **By Row** tool on the toolbar. Graph restores the display by rows.

WHY WORRY?

If the data labels won't fit after you switch from row to column display, click the graph, hold down the Ctrl key, and drag the right or left resize handle to expand the graph from the center.

NOTE ▼

Which is best? Column or row display? Sometimes, displaying by column doesn't make sense. Try it both ways. If displaying by column emphasizes the point you want to make, use it! If not, switch back to displaying by rows.

TASK 50

Adding or Removing Grid Lines

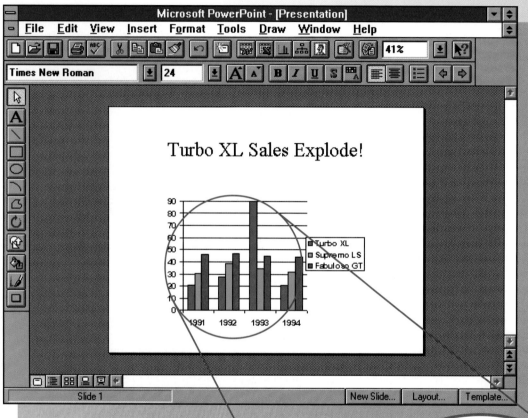

"Why would I do this?"

Some AutoFormat graphs include *grid lines*. These are horizontal and vertical lines within the graph body. They help your audience interpret the graph. You can turn the horizontal and vertical grid lines on or off manually, if you want. Turning off the grid lines makes for a less cluttered chart, but grid lines may help clarify the chart. Try turning them on and off to see which effect you like best.

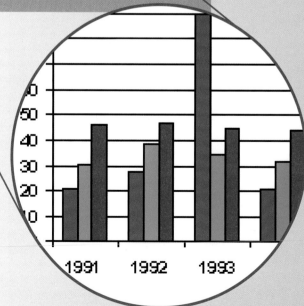

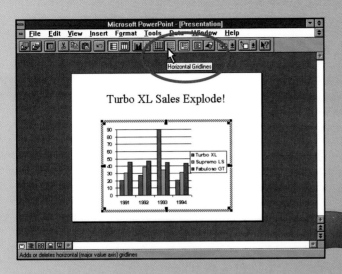

1 Use the chart you worked with in the previous task, or create a new chart. Double-click the chart to switch to Graph. Click the **Chart Type** tool on the toolbar to select the vertical bar chart type. With your chart displayed in the Graph window, click the **Horizontal Gridlines** tool on the toolbar to turn off the lines.

2 Now try turning on vertical gridlines by clicking the **Vertical Gridlines** tool on the toolbar. Before exiting Graph, turn off the vertical gridlines and turn on the horizontal gridlines by clicking the **Horizontal Gridline** tool on the toolbar.

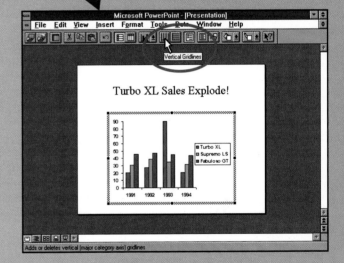

WHY WORRY?

To turn off gridlines, just click the Horizontal Gridlines or Vertical Gridlines tools on the toolbar again.

Removing the Legend

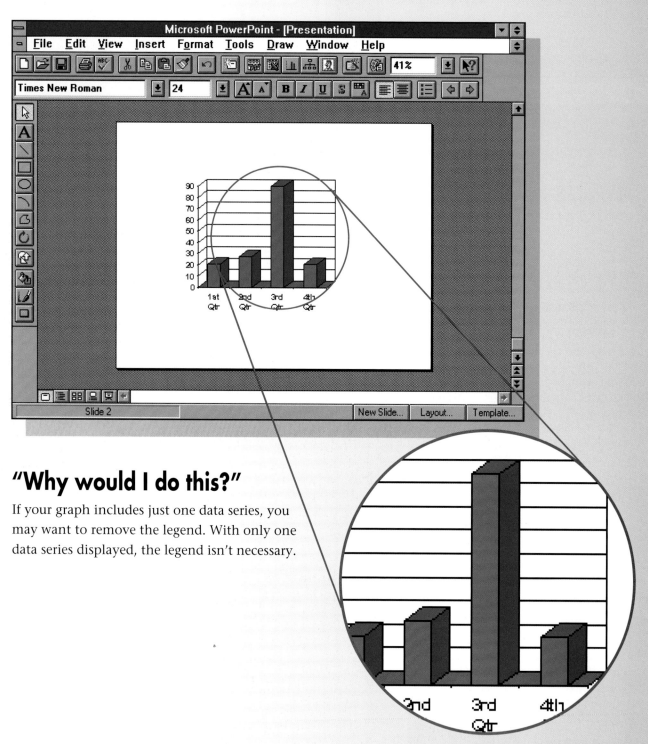

"Why would I do this?"

If your graph includes just one data series, you may want to remove the legend. With only one data series displayed, the legend isn't necessary.

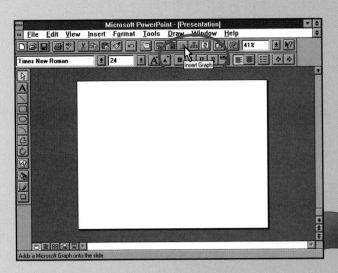

1 On a blank slide, click the **Insert Graph** tool on the toolbar to start a new graph.

2 With the datasheet displayed in the Graph window, click the row **2** button to select the row. Press and hold down **Shift** and click the row **3** button to select row 3 also. Press **Delete** to remove the data from the datasheet.

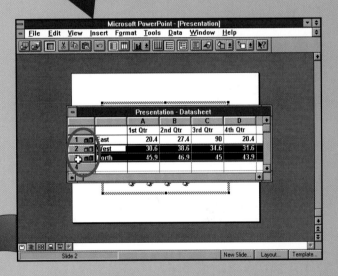

3 Click the **Legend** tool on the toolbar. The legend disappears. To exit Graph, click anywhere in the slide background.

TASK 52
Adding Explanatory Text

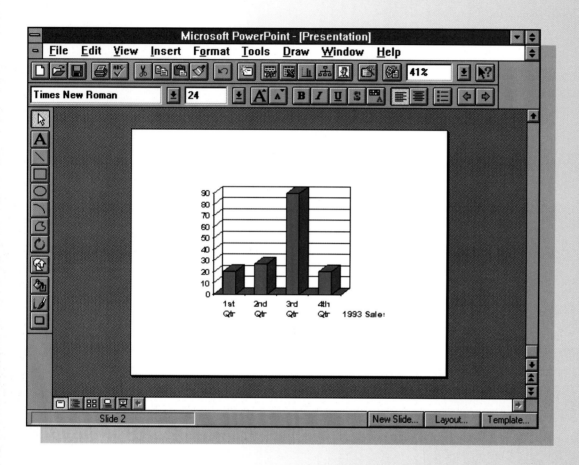

"Why would I do this?"

Your PowerPoint graphs should make their point clearly. To call your audience's attention to the data you want to emphasize, you can add explanatory text. You can use the text tool in the Graph window to add text anywhere on a graph. You may want to add title text above or below the graph to provide additional information. You also can use the Text tool to add descriptive labels anywhere on the graph.

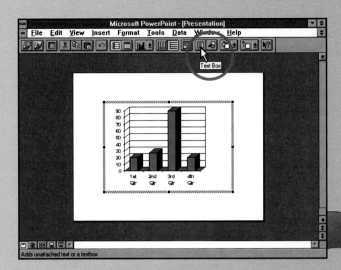

1 Double-click on any graph in your presentation to switch to Graph. With your graph displayed in the Graph window, click the **Text Box** tool on the toolbar. The pointer becomes a crosshair.

2 Click where you want the text to appear, and start typing. When you finish, click anywhere in the slide background to exit Graph.

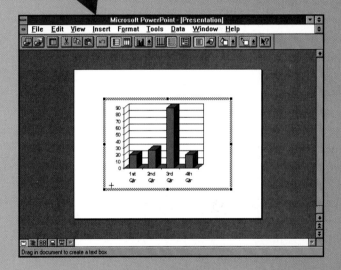

TASK 53
Adding Clip Art Anywhere

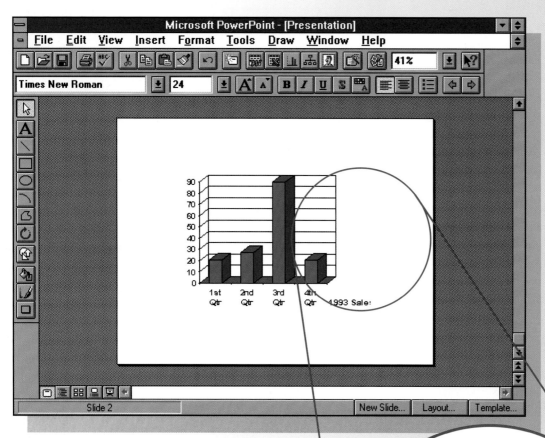

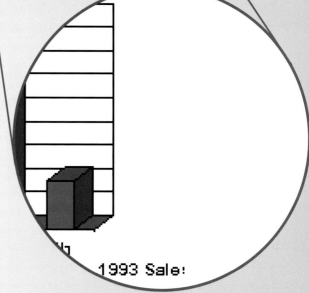

"Why would I do this?'

You don't have to be an artist to create good-looking artwork with PowerPoint. Begin with PowerPoint's library of clip art images, which you can add anywhere on a slide. You also can use PowerPoint's drawing tools to create simple illustrations, such as maps. If PowerPoint's drawing tools aren't sufficient for your needs, you can create a picture in a drawing program and then add it to your PowerPoint slide. You can insert clip art objects right on top of other objects, such as graphs. With clip art, you can turn an otherwise boring slide into an attention-grabber.

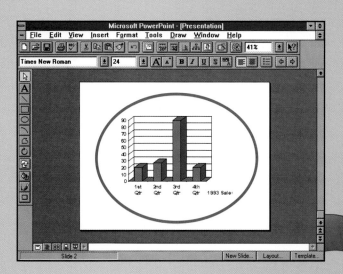

1 Display the slide to which you want to add clip art. Try adding clip art to a graph.

2 Click the **Insert Clip Art** tool on the toolbar. You see the ClipArt Gallery.

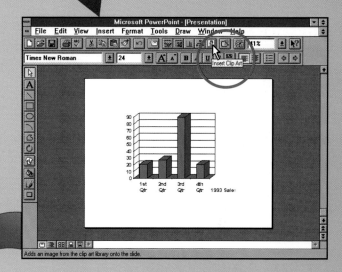

3 Choose a category from the list, and use the scroll bars to display and select the picture you want to insert.

165

4 Click OK to insert the clip art in your slide. If there are other objects where PowerPoint inserts the clip art, the clip-art object lies on top of them.

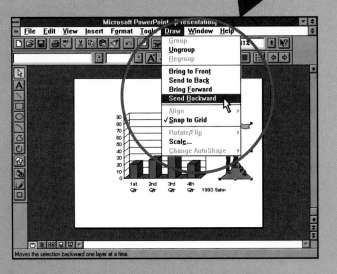

5 Move and resize the clip art object, if you want. If it covers other objects, try choosing **Send Backward** from the **Draw** menu.

WHY WORRY?

If you don't like the way the clip art looks, you can delete it. Press the Tab key until the object is selected, and press Delete.

Drawing Shapes

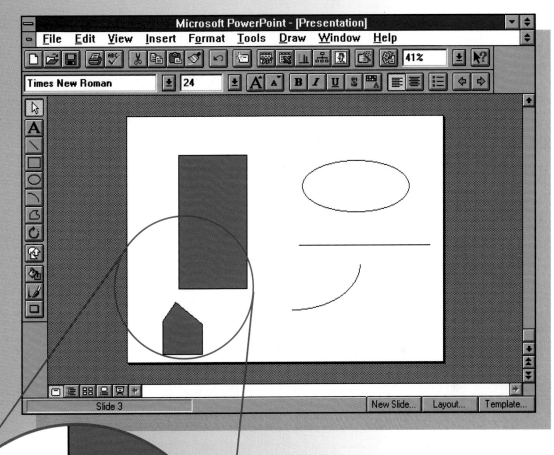

"Why would I do this?"

Sometimes you need a simple illustration to convey an idea visually. PowerPoint includes some basic drawing tools that help you create simple pictures. In this task, you learn how to work with rectangles and ovals. To create a simple illustration, you will need lines—straight lines, curved lines, and freeform lines. You also learn how to use PowerPoint's simple drawing tools to add these features to your slides.

Task 54: Drawing Shapes

1 On a blank slide, click the **Rectangle** tool on the toolbar. The pointer becomes a crosshair. On your slide, click and drag to create the rectangle. Release the mouse button when you are finished drawing the rectangle.

NOTE ▼

To create a perfect square, hold down the Shift key while you drag.

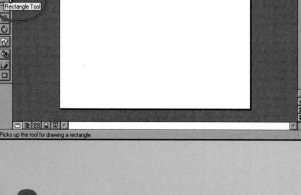

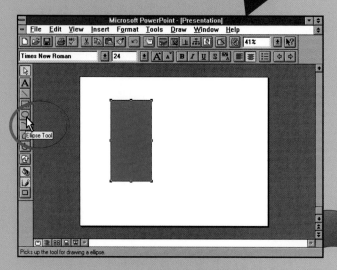

2 To draw an ellipse, click the **Ellipse** tool on the toolbar. Click and drag to create the oval. Release the mouse button when you are finished drawing the oval.

NOTE ▼

To create a perfect circle, hold down the Shift key while you drag.

3 When you add rectangles and ellipses, PowerPoint applies the default fill color for these shapes. If you want to remove the fill color, select the drawing object and click the **Fill On/Off** tool on the toolbar.

NOTE ▼

A drawing object is like any other object on a PowerPoint slide: You can select it individually, and you can perform actions such as sizing, copying, and choosing attributes.

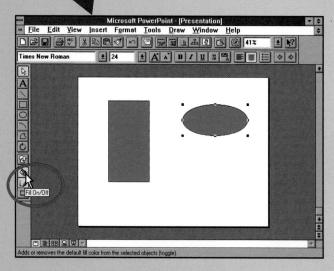

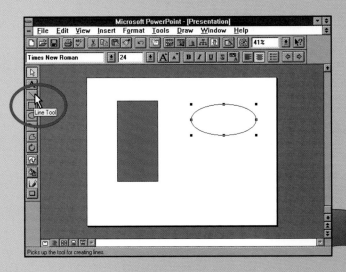

4 To draw a line, click the **Line** tool on the Drawing toolbar. The pointer becomes a crosshair. Click where you want the line to begin, and drag to draw the line. Release the mouse button when you are finished drawing the line.

> **NOTE** ▼
>
> To draw perfectly horizontal or vertical lines, or lines at a 45 degree angle, hold down the Shift key while dragging.

5 Now try creating an arc. Click the **Arc** tool on the Drawing toolbar, and click where you want the arc to begin. Try dragging in several directions to see what happens to the arc. When you are satisfied with the shape, release the mouse button.

> **NOTE** ▼
>
> You can also use the Freeform tool to create a freehand drawing. Just hold down the mouse button and drag. But don't get frustrated! Unless you have a very steady hand, the lines you draw will probably look jerky and rough.

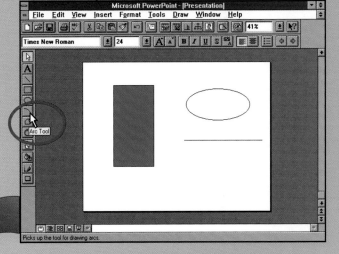

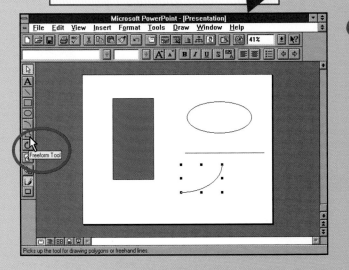

6 Now try creating a polygon with the Freeform tool. Click the **Freeform** tool on the Drawing toolbar, and click in your slide. Then move the pointer to another location, and click again. PowerPoint draws a straight line between the two points. When you are finished, double-click to stop drawing lines. If you enclose the polygon, PowerPoint applies the default fill color.

TASK 55
Adding a Picture

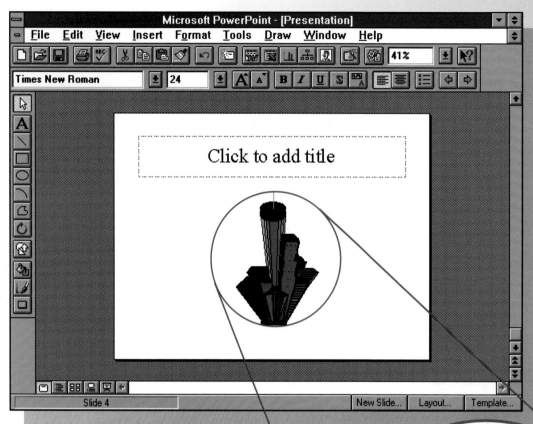

"Why would I do this?"

If you can't create the illustration you need with PowerPoint, you can insert a picture created by another graphics program. You can, for example, use clip art libraries other than the PowerPoint library. You also can insert photographs from CD-ROM disks.

In order to use your picture, the picture must have been saved in a *file format* that PowerPoint can recognize and use. Happily, PowerPoint recognizes almost all of the commonly used graphics file formats. If you don't know what these terms stand for, don't worry. If PowerPoint can read them, the program will recognize the format automatically.

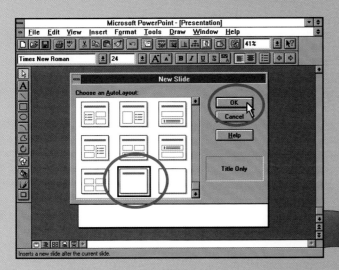

1 Add a new slide using the Title Only AutoLayout.

2 Choose **Picture** from the **Insert** menu. You see the Insert Picture dialog box. Use the Drives and Directories lists to display the disk or directory that contains the picture you want to add.

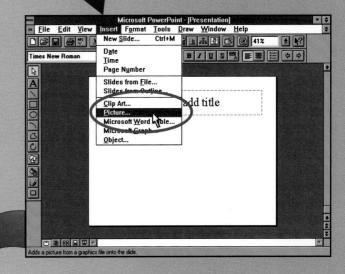

3 In the **File name** drop-down list box, double-click the name of the file you want to add or click the file name and then click **OK**. PowerPoint inserts the picture as an object on your slide.

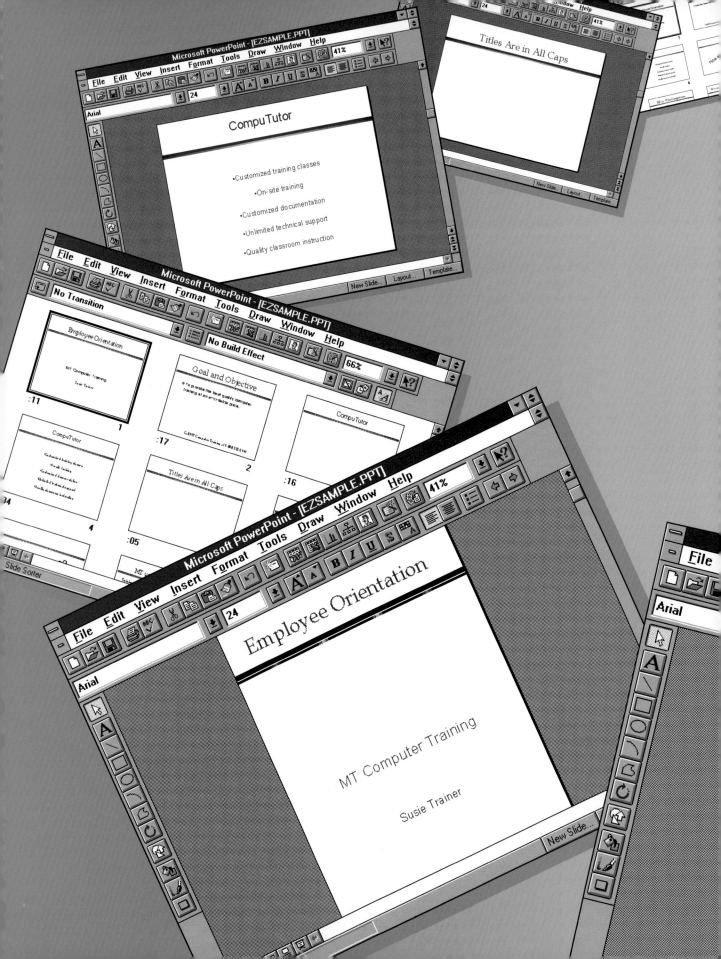

PART VI

Fine-Tuning Your Presentation and Producing Media

After you finish creating your slides, you are ready to make sure your presentation meets professional standards. With Slide Sorter, you can make sure your slides are in the correct order—and if they're not, you easily can rearrange them. With the Change Case command, you easily can correct problems with inconsistent capitalization. With PowerPoint's spelling checker, you can make sure that your presentation does not contain an embarrassing spelling mistake. PowerPoint even will time your presentation so that you won't risk getting cut off if you run over your allotted time.

presntation
^
e

With PowerPoint, you can produce a variety of presentation media. The simplest and least expensive, requiring no special equipment other than your printer, is to print your slides on paper. You also can print your outline, speaker's notes, and audience handouts on paper.

For a more professional-looking presentation, consider producing overhead transparencies, a computer slide show, or 35mm slides.

- **Overheads** If you have a laser or inkjet printer, you can load it with transparencies specially made for laser printers, such as 3M Scotch Laser Printer Transparencies or 3M Inkjet Printer Transparencies (for Hewlett-Packard DeskJets). You print on these transparencies as if they were paper. The result is a set of high-quality transparencies you can project using an overhead projector.

- **Slide Show (Electronic Presentation)** A *slide show* is an electronic presentation that utilizes your computer. Your slides fill the screen, and you can use a variety of special effects, such as timings, transitions, and builds. To display your slide show, you can use a desktop computer—but only for a small audience of, at the most, three or four persons. For a larger audience, you'll need a *projection panel*. This is a transparent color computer display designed to fit on top of an overhead projector.

■ **35mm Slides** If you can fully darken the room in which you are going to give your presentation, you can present colorful 35mm slides. Simply save your PowerPoint presentation to a floppy disk, and give or send the disk to a graphics service bureau. This is the best choice for a large audience because you can project the slides onto a large screen. Be forewarned, however; you will need ample lead time. If one or more of the slides did not turn out or contain mistakes, you will have to reshoot them and have them developed again.

Whichever output medium you choose, the process you follow to produce output is the same. First, select the printer you want to use, and then you open the presentation you want to print. Next, you set up your slides by choosing the output media and orientation (portrait or landscape). Finally, you choose the command that starts producing output.

TASK 56

Reordering Slides in Slide Sorter

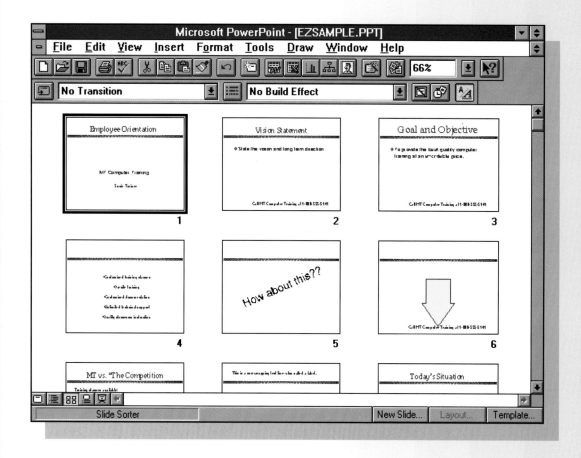

"Why would I do this?"

Before the computer, graphics professionals organized their presentations with a *light table*. This was a box with a light inside and a translucent plastic top. When you put your 35mm slides on the top of the box, you could see the slides' contents. PowerPoint's Slide Sorter works (and looks) exactly like a light table. It enables you to see your slides and rearrange them.

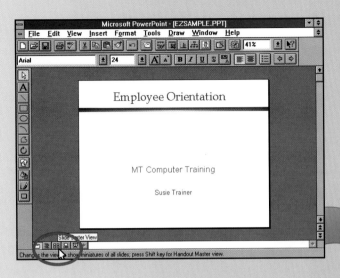

1 Open a presentation that contains some practice slides, and click the **Slide Sorter** tool (on the bottom window border). In the Slide Sorter window, note that one slide is selected.

2 Click the slide and drag to the left, to the right, down, and up. As you do, note the dotted line that appears. This shows you where Slide Sorter will move the slide when you release the mouse button.

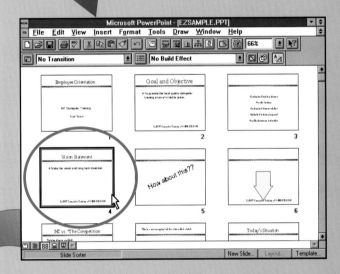

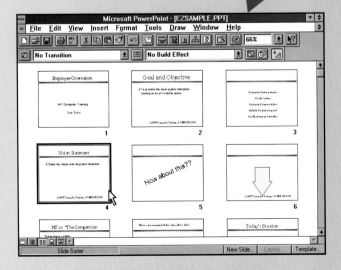

3 Release the mouse button to complete the move.

WHY WORRY?

You can undo any action you perform in the Slide Sorter, including moving and deleting slides. Just click the Undo button.

Task 56: Reordering Slides in Slide Sorter

4 To select another slide, just click it. To get a closer look at a slide, just double-click it. PowerPoint switches to Slide view and displays the slide. To get back to Slide Sorter, just click the **Slide Sorter** button.

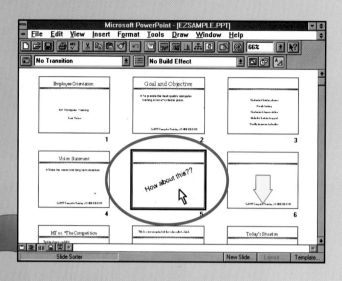

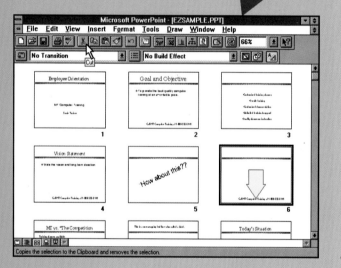

5 To delete a slide, select the slide then press **Delete**. Try this, and then immediately click the **Undo** tool on the toolbar to restore the deletion.

> **NOTE** ▼
>
> You can create new and duplicate slides in the Slide Sorter, if you want. To create a new slide, select the slide that you want to come before the new slide, and click the Slide Sorter button. To duplicate a slide, select the slide, and choose Duplicate from the Edit menu.

Consistency in Capitalization

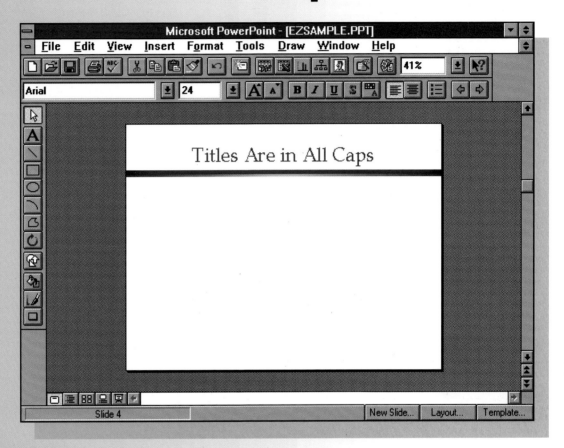

"Why would I do this?"

A common error in amateur presentations is to use capitalization inconsistently in slide titles, subtitles, and bulleted lists. Be a pro! Proofread your presentation carefully to ensure that there are no inconsistencies in the way you have used capitalization. Check your presentation in Slide view, not Outline view. If you find errors in capitalization, don't bother to correct them manually. You can use the Change Case command to make the correction automatically.

Task 57: Consistency in Capitalization

1 On one of your practice slides, type a title with inconsistent capitalization, and select the title.

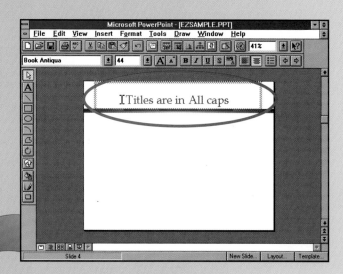

2 Choose **Change Case** from the **Format** menu. You see the Change Case dialog box.

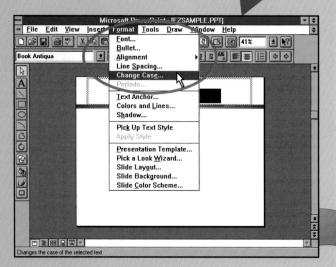

WHY WORRY?

The Change Case command is "smart" enough to follow accepted capitalization rules. The Title option, for example, does not capitalize prepositions unless they appear at the beginning of the title. The Change Case command only works on the current slide. You must repeat the process for additional slides.

3 Choose the case option you want. The examples in the dialog box show what each option will do. Click **OK** after you make your choice. PowerPoint makes the correction.

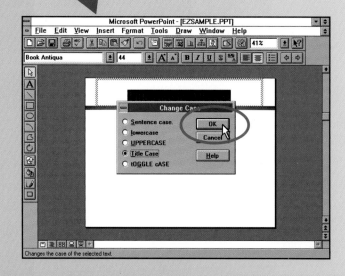

Checking Spelling

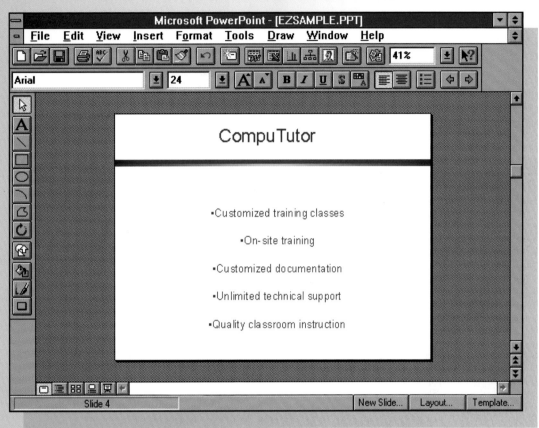

"Why would I do this?"

Have you ever seen a presentation that contained spelling mistakes? The mistakes reflect poorly on the speaker. Be sure to check your spelling before you go on stage. PowerPoint's Spelling command checks the spelling throughout your presentation, including speaker's notes, outlines, and the text in your slides' text objects (such as titles and bulleted lists).

Task 58: Checking Spelling

1 In an existing slide, switch to Slide view, and click the **Spelling** tool. PowerPoint immediately begins checking the spelling of your presentation. If Spelling finds a word that it can't match in its dictionary, you see the Spelling dialog box.

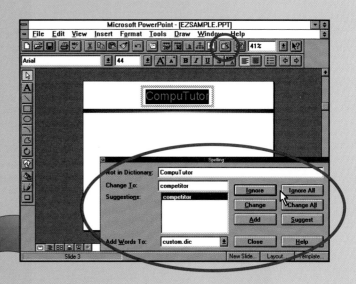

NOTE ▼

Don't check spelling in Outline view. If you do, PowerPoint won't check the spelling in any side-by-side bulleted lists you may have inserted. PowerPoint also can't check the spelling of words that are part of objects.

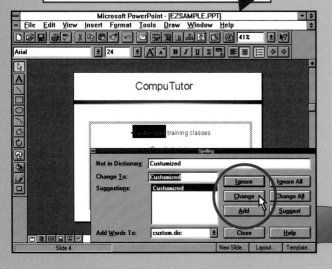

2 Click **Ignore** to skip the word this time; click **Ignore All** to skip this word throughout the presentation. Click **Add** if the word is correctly spelled; this adds the word to the dictionary.

WHY WORRY?

PowerPoint's dictionary does not contain many proper nouns (the names of people and places). Be sure to add commonly used proper nouns to the Spelling dictionary.

3 When Spelling finds an incorrectly spelled word, shows spelling suggestions in the Suggestions list. Highlight the correct spelling, and click **Change** or **Change All** (to make the change throughout your presentation). If Spelling cannot locate the correct spelling, type the correct spelling in the **Change To** box, and click **Change** or **Change All**.

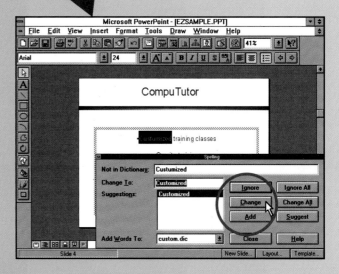

Rehearsing Your Presentation

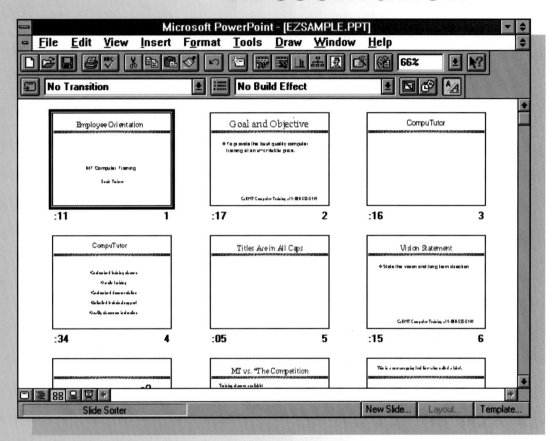

"Why would I do this?"

Your audience expects you to stick to your allotted time. In a busy conference, you may be yanked off the podium if you go over your limit! PowerPoint can help you rehearse your presentation by timing how long you spend on each slide. This is a great feature and one you should use every time!

Task 59: Rehearsing Your Presentation

1 Open the presentation you want to rehearse and click the **Slide Sorter** tool to switch to Slide Sorter. If you haven't finished your "real" presentation, just use some practice slides to see how this works.

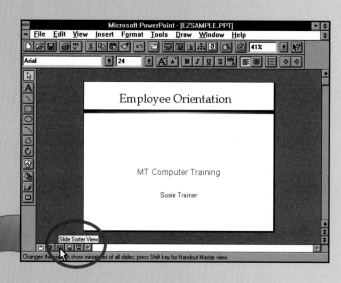

2 Click the **Rehearse Timing** button. You see a full-screen version of your first slide. Make your remarks about this slide. When you are ready to go on to the next slide, click the **Timing** button at the bottom left corner of the screen.

NOTE ▼

Don't spend too long on a slide. Your audience's attention may wander. If you find yourself talking for more than two or three minutes about a slide, make two or more slides for this subject.

3 After you click the Timing button on the last slide, you see the Slide Sorter dialog box. It gives the total elapsed time for your presentation. If you want to record the slide timings in the Slide Sorter dialog box, click **Yes**.

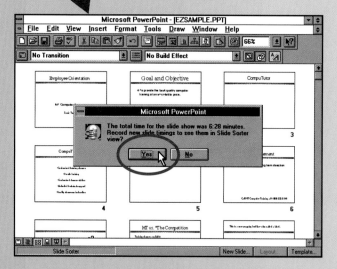

Setting Up the Slides

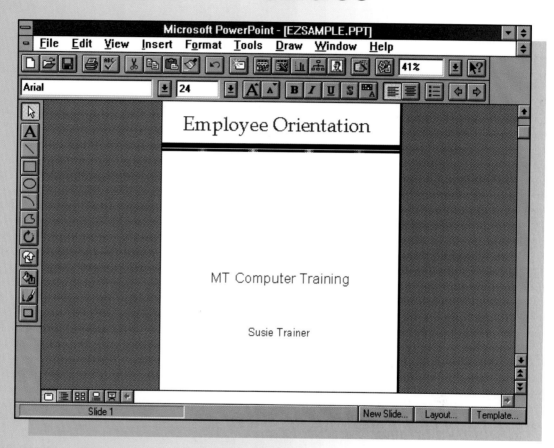

"Why would I do this?"

Before you produce output, set up your slides by telling PowerPoint what type of output you intend to produce. You can choose from on-screen slide show (electronic presentation), letter-sized paper, A4 (European) paper, 35mm slides, and custom sizes. If you want to print overheads, you should choose one of the paper sizes (letter or A4).

Task 60: Setting Up the Slides

1 Choose **Slide Setup** from the **File** menu. You see the Slide Setup dialog box.

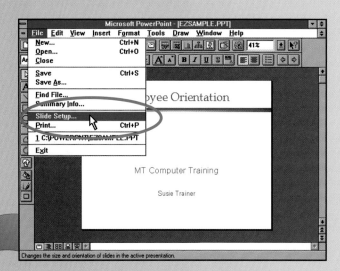

2 In the **Slides Sized For** drop-down list box, choose one of the options. For an electronic presentation, choose **On-screen Show**. If you are printing overheads, choose **Letter Paper (U.S.)** or **A4 Paper(Europe)**. If you want to produce 35mm slides, choose this option.

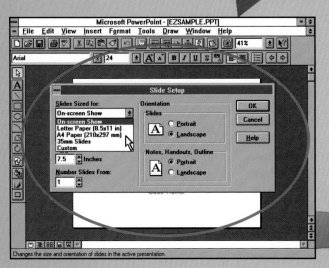

WHY WORRY?

Looking for the Overheads option? Choose one of the paper options (letter or A4).

3 If you want to print overheads, click **Portrait** in the Slides area. Some overhead projectors will clip off the sides of your transparencies if you choose Landscape orientation. Click **OK** to confirm your slide setup choices. PowerPoint adjusts your slides to reflect the changes you have made.

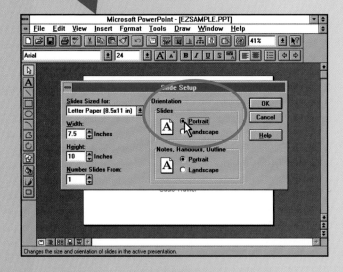

Printing Your Presentation

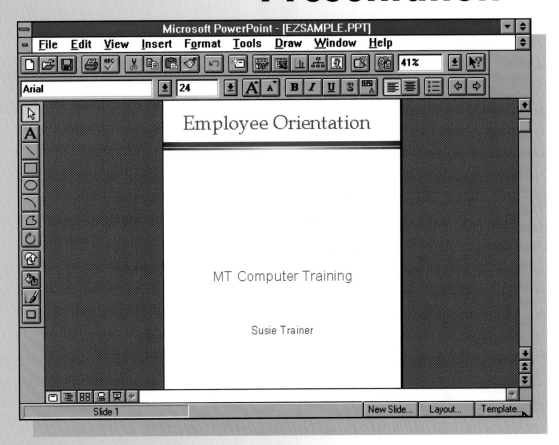

"Why would I do this?"

You can print your entire presentation, including your slides, speaker's notes, outline, and audience handouts. The handouts are printed copies of your slides, grouped two, three, or six per page.

You easily can produce presentation media inexpensively by using laser transparencies. These are clear sheets, the size of paper, that you load into your printer as if they were ordinary paper. You also can get transparencies for inkjet printers. If you want to use these, load your printer with the transparencies now.

Task 61: Printing Your Presentation

1 Choose **Print** from the **File** menu. You see the Print dialog box.

NOTE ▼

If you plan to print audience handouts, try the 2-per-page option. This gives plenty of room for notes.

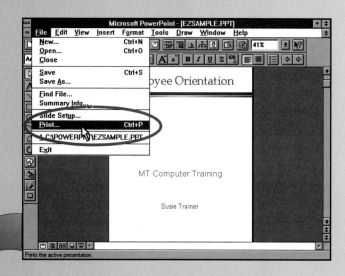

2 In the **Print What** box, choose the output you want PowerPoint to produce. The program can print your slides (on paper or laser transparencies), Notes Pages, Handouts (2, 3, or 6 slides per page), or the Outline View.

NOTE ▼

The Print tool bypasses the Print dialog box. If you click this button, PowerPoint starts printing all your slides.

3 If you want to print just part of your presentation, choose an option in the Slide Range area. You can print the currently-selected slide (the one that's visible in Slide view or selected in Outline or Slide Sorter view). You also can print a range of slides by typing a range (such as *2-7*) in the text box. Click **OK** to start printing your presentation, with the choices you've made.

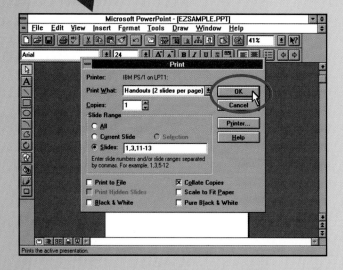

Running a
Slide Show

Goal and Objective

- To provide the **best** quality computer training at an **affordable** price.

Call MT Computer Training at 1-800-555-5141

"Why would I do this?"

Perhaps the best way to give a PowerPoint presentation is to create an electronic presentation on-screen. Your slides will appear in vivid color. You can use the mouse pointer to point out features of your slides. You can even draw and write on the screen.

Task 62: Running a Slide Show

1 Open a presentation. (A practice presentation will do.) Switch to Slide Sorter by clicking the **Slide Sorter** tool, and click the first slide.

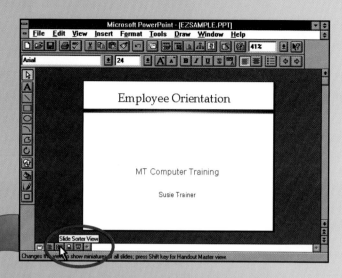

2 Click the **Slide Show** tool. This is one of the view tools at the bottom of the window. PowerPoint zooms the slide so that it takes over the screen.

3 To advance to the next slide, click the mouse button, or press **spacebar** (or the **N** key, **PgDn**, **right arrow**, or **down arrow**). To view the previous slide, click the right mouse button or press **Backspace** (or **P**).

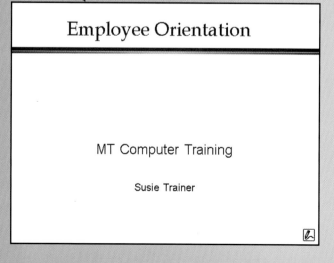

Employee Orientation

MT Computer Training

Susie Trainer

4 To write or draw on the screen with the mouse, click the **Freehand Annotation** tool—the pencil icon in the lower right corner of the screen. Click and hold down the mouse button to write or draw. When you are finished, click the **Freehand Annotation** tool again to restore the mouse pointer.

5 Continue until you have viewed all the slides. To stop viewing before reaching the last slide, just press **Esc**. You see Slide Sorter again.

WHY WORRY?

The writing or drawing you make this way is temporary; it does not affect the slide's appearance after the slide show is over.

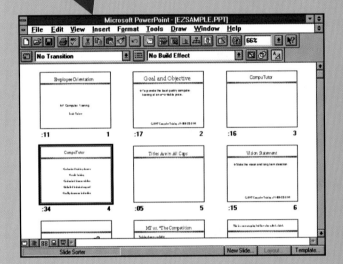

TASK 63

Adding Builds and Transitions

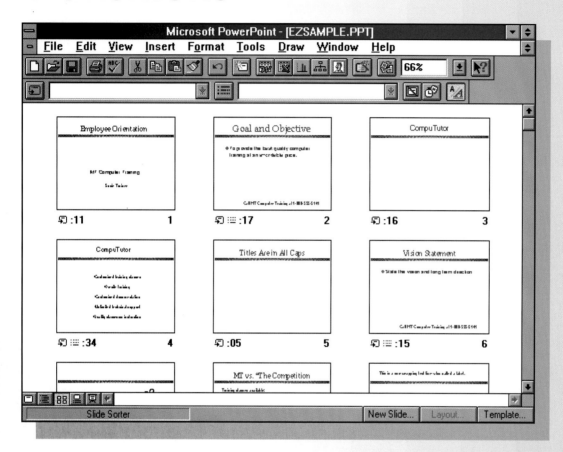

"Why would I do this?"

When you present an electronic slide show, you can take advantage of advanced presentation features called *builds* and *transitions*. A build is very useful for adding drama and interest to bulleted list charts. A build transforms the chart into several charts, each of which adds an item in the list until the whole list is complete. A transition is a special effect that adds visual interest as you go from one slide and to the next.

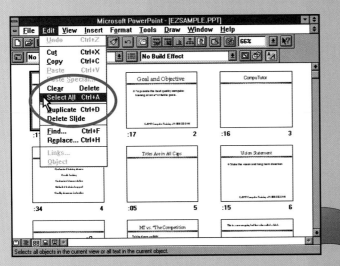

1 In Slide Sorter view, choose **Selects All** from the **Edit** menu or press **Ctrl+A** to select all the slides.

2 Now click the arrow next to the Transition Effects list box. Choose **Random Transition** from the list. This gives a variety of effects as you move from slide to slide. In the Slide Sorter window, you see icons next to each slide. These icons indicate that a transition has been chosen for the slide.

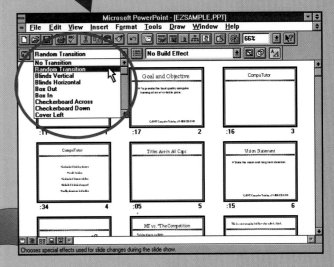

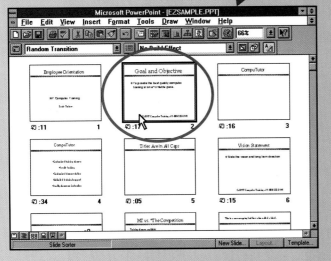

3 Click any space between slides to deselect the slides. Click the first bulleted list slide. Then press and hold down **Shift** while you select the rest of the bulleted list slides in your presentation.

Task 63: Adding Builds and Transitions

4 From the Build Effects list box, choose **Random Effects**. You see an icon under these slides. This indicates that builds have been chosen.

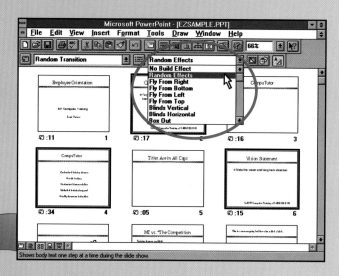

5 Now click the **Slide Show** tool to see what your slide show looks like with these professional-looking effects!

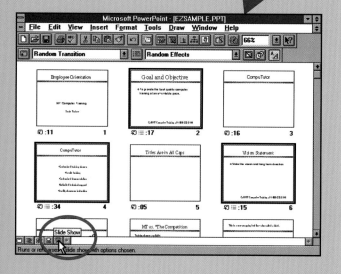

Software Training

- Professional instructors and individualized attention
- Train with equipment similar to your own
- Classes scheduled for your convenience
- Text books and disks included
- Discount on second class

Laser Printers

- Shark TL-600
  - 600 DPI
  - PostScript compatible
  - 8 PPM
  - 2 M RAM
- Spirit DT-300
  - 300 DPI
  - HP PCL4
  - 4 PPM
  - 1 M RAM

- Quirk 600234
  - 600 DPI
  - PostScript compatible
  - 6 PPM
  - 2 M RAM
- Com-D 2
  - 300 DPI
  - PostScript compatible
  - 6 PPM
  - 2 M RAM

LISTEN TO THE MUSIC

CLASSIFICATION	ARTIST	TITLE	CD	TAPE
Chicago Blues	Willie Rush			
	Ray King	Ain't I Right	X	X
		King's Blues	X	X
Texas Blues	T-Bone Green			
	The Governors	Green's R&B	X	X
Zydeco		Not Quite		
	Queen Mills		X	X
	Boogie 'n' Bob	Cookin'		
		Boogie Down	X	X

One of our Favorites

First Quarter Sales 1994

25000

20000

15000

10000

5000

0   Jan.   Feb.   Mar.   A

PART VII

Sample Documents

- ▼ Add Bullets and Formatting for Emphasis

- ▼ Create a Slide Using Clip Art and the Pick a Look Wizard

- ▼ Add a Table and an AutoShape to a Slide

- ▼ Add a Bar Graph to a Slide

- ▼ Use Fills, Patterns, and Objects in a Presentation

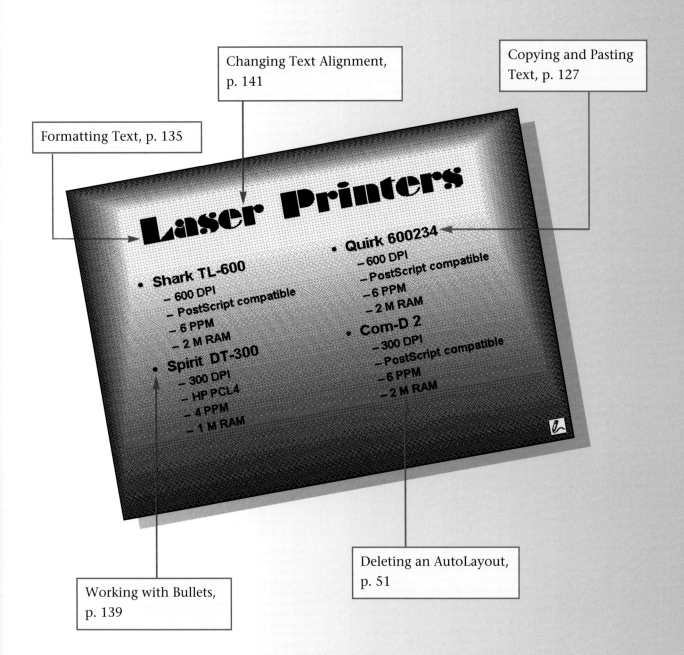

Changing Text Alignment, p. 141

Copying and Pasting Text, p. 127

Formatting Text, p. 135

Working with Bullets, p. 139

Deleting an AutoLayout, p. 51

Add Bullets and Formatting for Emphasis

1 Type the two levels of bullet text. See this task for help:

Working with Bullets   *Task 43, p. 139*

2 Copy the bullet text and paste it beside the first bulleted list. See this task on copying and pasting text:

Copying and Pasting Text   *Task 39, p. 127*

3 Substitute a different background for the AutoLayout. See this task:

Deleting an AutoLayout   *Task 13, p. 51*

4 Change the font and font size. See the following task for information:

Formatting Text   *Task 42, p. 135*

5 Center the title text for variety. See this task:

Changing Text Alignment   *Task 44, p. 141*

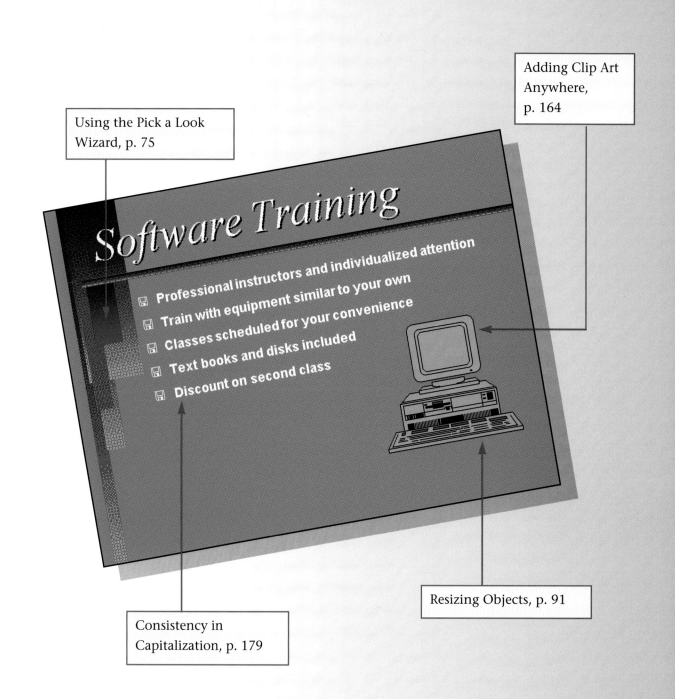

Using the Pick a Look Wizard, p. 75

Adding Clip Art Anywhere, p. 164

Consistency in Capitalization, p. 179

Resizing Objects, p. 91

Create a Slide Using Clip Art and the Pick a Look Wizard

1 Change the background of one slide or the entire presentation. For help on this task, see:

Using the Pick a Look Wizard   *Task 20, p. 75*

2 Insert clip art from PowerPoint or other programs. For more information, see these tasks:

Adding Clip Art Anywhere   *Task 53, p. 164*
Adding a Picture   *Task 55, p. 170*

3 Reduce or enlarge clip art or a picture. See this task:

Resizing Objects   *Task 24, p. 91*

4 Use the change case command to make your capitalization consistent. See this task:

Consistency in Capitalization   *Task 57, p. 179*

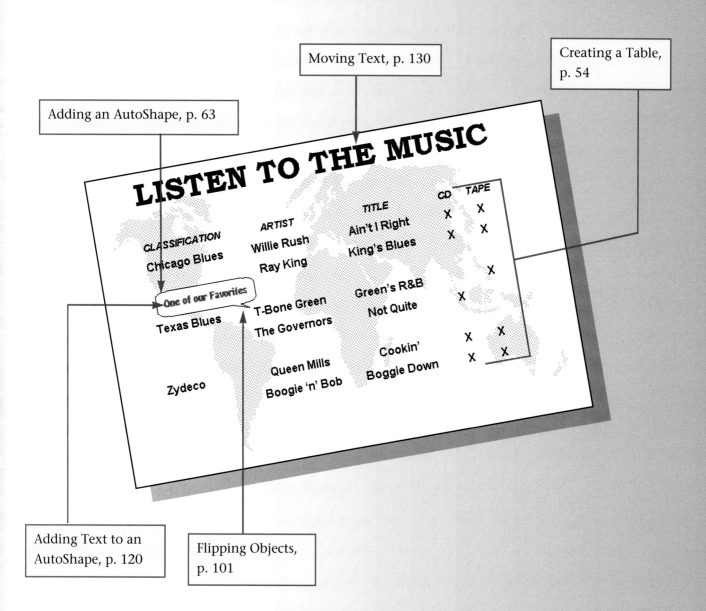

Moving Text, p. 130

Creating a Table, p. 54

Adding an AutoShape, p. 63

Adding Text to an AutoShape, p. 120

Flipping Objects, p. 101

Add a Table and an AutoShape to a Slide

1 Insert a Microsoft Word table to organize information in your presentation. See this task for help:

> *Creating a Table*   *Task 14, p. 54*

2 Add any of various shapes to your document, including a cartoon callout box. See this task to add a shape:

> *Adding an AutoShape*   *Task 16, p. 63*

3 Flip an object, picture, clip art, or AutoShape horizontally or vertically. See this task:

> *Flipping Objects*   *Task 29, p. 101*

4 Insert text into any AutoShape or other object. See this task for help:

> *Adding Text to an AutoShape*   *Task 36, p. 120*

5 Move text to any position on the page. See this task for information:

> *Moving Text*   *Task 40, p. 130*

Adding or Removing Grid Lines, p. 158

Adding a Graph Anywhere, p. 152

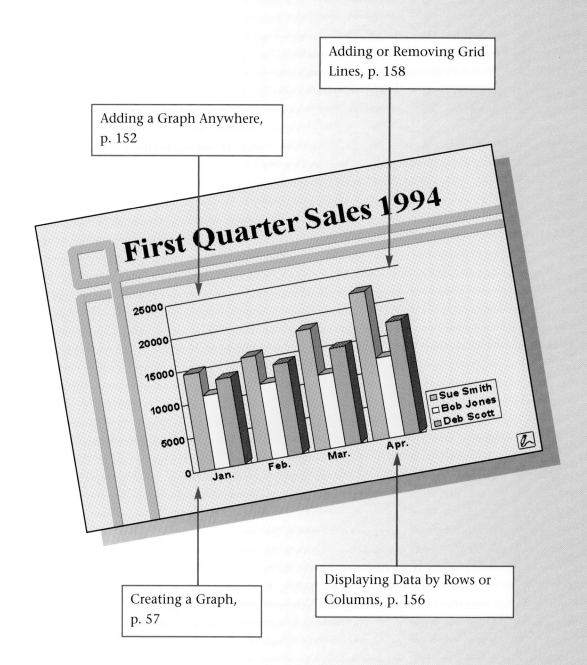

Creating a Graph, p. 57

Displaying Data by Rows or Columns, p. 156

Add a Bar Graph to a Slide

1 Choose the graph type, enter the data, and create the graph type. See this task for help:

Creating a Graph   Task 15, p. 57

2 Add a graph on any page and in any location. See this task for help:

Adding a Graph Anywhere   Task 47, p. 152

3 Choose how to display the data by switching row titles with column titles. See this task for more information:

Displaying Data by Rows   Task 49, p. 156
or Columns

4 Add vertical or horizontal grid lines, or both. See the following task for more information:

Adding or Removing Grid Lines   Task 50, p. 158

Part VII: Sample Documents

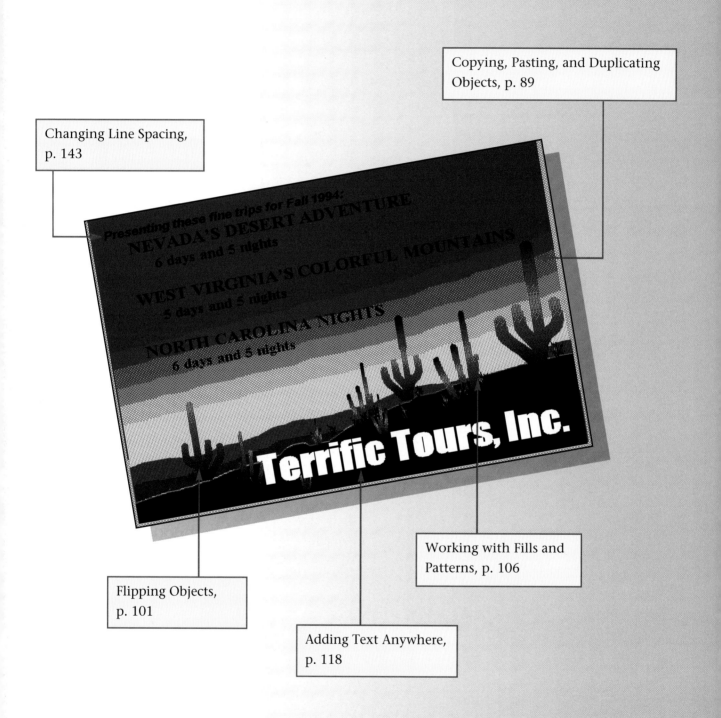

Copying, Pasting, and Duplicating Objects, p. 89

Changing Line Spacing, p. 143

Working with Fills and Patterns, p. 106

Flipping Objects, p. 101

Adding Text Anywhere, p. 118

Presenting these fine trips for Fall 1994:
NEVADA'S DESERT ADVENTURE
6 days and 5 nights

WEST VIRGINIA'S COLORFUL MOUNTAINS
5 days and 5 nights

NORTH CAROLINA NIGHTS
6 days and 5 nights

Terrific Tours, Inc.

Use Fills, Patterns, and Objects in a Presentation

1 Duplicate objects so that the picture is more interesting. For more information, see this task:

Copying, Pasting, and Duplicating Objects   *Task 23, p. 89*

2 After copying and pasting an object, flip it so that it looks different from the other objects. See this task for help:

Flipping Objects   *Task 29, p. 101*

3 Choose various colors, shading, and patterns to fill objects. See this topic for more information about fills:

Working with Fills and Patterns   *Task 31, p. 106*

4 Reduce spacing between lines of text. See this task for help:

Changing Line Spacing   *Task 45, p. 143*

5 You can add text to anywhere on the page. See this task for information about adding text:

Adding Text Anywhere   *Task 35, p. 118*

Glossary

attribute   An aspect of an object's appearance, such as fill color, patterns, or borders.

AutoFormat   In Microsoft Graph, a chart type—such as a bar or pie chart—that includes preset fonts, grids, legends, and other formats.

AutoLayout   A predesigned slide layout you choose when you create a new slide. AutoLayouts have placeholders for objects, such as titles, graphs, and clip art.

AutoShape   A shape, such as an arrow, that you can enter into your drawing and size as you want.

border   The lines around an object.

build   In electronic presentations, a special effect for bulleted lists. The first slide shows the first item in the bulleted list, while the second slide shows the second item, and so on.

clip art   Pictures you can add to your presentation to add visual spice. PowerPoint comes with a large library of clip-art images.

constrain   To force PowerPoint to draw, move, or size an object in a straight horizontal, vertical, or 45-degree angled path.

data series   A collection of data about one item, such as the sales for the Eastern region for each month in 1994.

datasheet   In Microsoft Graph, the spreadsheet-like window in which you enter your data. Put each data series in a row, and add column headings.

fill color   The color of an object's background.

grid   An invisible criss-crossed web of horizontal and vertical lines on a slide. When the Snap To Grid option is turned on (Draw menu), these lines "attract" objects that you place on-screen by dragging.

group   To link two or more objects so that they can be selected and edited as if they were one object.

guides   Horizontal and vertical lines that you can use to position and align objects. When you drag objects on-screen and release the mouse button, they "snap" to the nearest guide that is visible on-screen. You can drag the guides to position them. To turn on the guides, choose Guides from the View menu.

object   An area set aside to hold a certain type of information, such as text, a graph, clip art, or a drawing. Each object can be independently selected and moved.

placeholder   In an AutoLayout, an area that you can double-click to enter a particular type of object, such as clip art, a table, or a graph.

regroup   To restore the links among objects that were formerly grouped so that you can select and edit them as if they were one object.

resize handle   A square that appears at each corner, and in the middle of each border, of a selected object. By dragging the resize handles, you can change the size of an object.

stacked objects   Objects placed on top of one another on-screen. The most recently added object is on "top" of the stack. You can send objects backwards and forwards. In order to see objects beneath the stack, you may need to send the top object backwards.

table   A set of boxes, two or more columns wide in each row, in which you can type words and numbers. As you type, the box automatically expands to accommodate your text.

Text tool   A tool on the Drawing toolbar that enables you to add text wherever you want. If you click this tool and then click a slide, you can type a line of text. If you click this tool and drag a box, you can type text that will word-wrap within the box.

ungroup   To break the links between two or more grouped objects so that they can be independently selected and edited.

Index

Index

Index